The Art of Compromise

Aural Piano Tuning

SPECIAL EDITION

By James Musselwhite

The Art of Compromise
Aural Piano Tuning

Library of Congress Cataloguing in Publication Data

Synopsis:
An introduction to the Art of Piano Tuning by ear.
Musselwhite, James E.
The Art of Compromise – Special Edition
1. How-To – Guides, Information, etc.
2. Music - Piano, Piano Technicians, Piano Technical,
etc.
I. Title.

ISBN-13: 978-1985648593
ISBN-10: 1985648598

James Musselwhite

My thanks to the following teachers:

Robert Lowrey
Dick Lewis
Gordon Fishwick
George Diefenbaugh
Mrs. Robinson
David Ferguson
Hugo Spilker
Grant Smalley
Nikolai Svinarenko
Earl Ewing
John Musselwhite
All My Clients
and...
my Father.

Table of Contents

Preface

Don't be afraid, be informed. A piano can't hurt you unless it falls on you (SO DON'T MOVE ONE YOURSELF!), and it could be one of the best friends you'll ever have.

What does the word "piano" mean to you? To most people, it conjures up an image of something that is familiar and unfamiliar at the same time. They have seen a piano on a stage, or in a home, but they have never owned one, or even played one.

To me, this is a remarkable fact. I grew up around pianos, and interact with them daily - but even though they are everywhere, the fact is that many think of a piano as something that someone else uses, that other people own.

However, they are a universal and accessible instrument. To play a piano, all you have to do is press a key.

This is a little handbook for those wanting to learn how to tune, or wanting to improve their tuning skills. Before you pick up this book, you should ask yourself four simple questions:

1. Is this something I am or could be passionate about?

2. Do I love music, and music making?

3. Am I the type of person who likes to work independently, yet enjoys dealing with people?

4. Do I have the patience and time to commit to learning a challenging skill?

If you answered yes to the majority of these questions, and are mechanically inclined with good problem-solving skills, then I encourage you to press ahead.

Piano tuning is a handy and interesting skill to have. You can use it to make pocket money, or a full-time income. However, to be a bad piano tuner is a sacrilege. As professionals we strive to not only be good at what we do, but educate the public as well. To tune a piano poorly in order to make "a quick buck" is not only cheating the customer out of their money, but also robbing them of the experience of having a properly tuned instrument. This can cause students to lose interest, owners to lose trust, and fellow tuners to lose respect.

To be a professional piano tuner, you must strive to be as skilled, honest, and informative as possible.

Even if you are just starting out, I would encourage you to join the Piano Technicians Guild. Not only is it a top-notch source of education and support, but the PTG also tests and accredits new tuners. Associating yourself with the PTG will ensure that you can reach your goal. Having the support, encouragement, and help of fellow tuners is the only way to make sure that you are upholding the highest standards in this field.

James (Jamie) Musselwhite.

Foreword

Tuning a piano is a skill, a craft and an art. Knowing how to tune, tuning, and understanding tuning are three completely separate things. My father patiently demonstrated to me how to tune, but it took a long time to learn how to do it myself. It took an even longer time to really understand, and be comfortable with it.

There are many skills that have to be learned to tune a piano accurately, but there are just three basic parts to each tuning. The first, and the most important from a tuner's point of view, is called "Setting the temperament". This is the foundation on which the rest of the tuning is built, and the hardest part to master. It is also rather difficult to explain.

The musical scale that Western ears have become accustomed to, and upon which the tuning of a piano is based, consists of twelve notes: C, C#, D, D#, E, F, F#, G, G#, A, A#, and B. This arrangement had been invented and used long before any of the composers we know of had been born. So, when they did get here, they inherited a system of music that they were forced to use, even though it has a few nasty little problems.

The main problem has its root in something called harmonics. If you play a string, and then divide it in half by placing your finger on the middle of the string (what physicists call "the node"), you would hear a note one octave higher than the first note, which is called the "Fundamental". (If you play middle C on a piano, and the C above it that is in tune, that is an octave.) If you then divide that half in half again, you would hear a 'Perfect Fifth' above the octave. (Like playing C and the G above it.) If you continued to subdivide the string in this manner, you would hear a rather mysterious thing: a note two octaves higher, then a third (C to E) above that. Then the fifth, then a minor 7th (C to A#), then all the diatonic notes (like all the white keys), and then every single note. If you could go even further you would hear microtones, which are not part of the western scale, but which are a part of the music of other cultures.

This is all fine and dandy, except for a problem known as the "Pythagorean Comma". The first interval of a perfect fifth in harmonics is "pure"; that is to say, it does not have any warble or vibrato, called "beats", when the two notes, the fundamental and the fifth, are played together. All the intervals after this are also "pure" with the note previous to it, but they grow increasingly sharp of the fundamental to the point that the octaves are not "pure" with each other. They become sharp because of the "Comma", which is a microtone that is missing in our western scale. So, in effect, we actually squeeze what is harmonically thirteen notes into our twelve-note scale. This is called "tempering" the scale, and the way in which we squeeze it is called the "temperament".

When there were no keyboard instruments, this was not a big problem. Instrumentalists and singers learned to tune each note as they played or sang, so that they would be pure to any other notes played or sung with them. Since pianos and other keyboard instruments cannot be re-tuned on the fly, dealing with this became a problem that no one has really been able to solve completely.

Before J.S. Bach's time, harpsichordists dealt with the problem of temperament by constantly tuning. They would play a piece in say, E flat, and then re-tune the instrument to play in a different key, like A or D. Large pipe organs of the time would have different temperaments in separate sets of pipes, called "ranks". To play in a different key, you would change ranks. This method of changing temperaments was not only awkward, but still resulted in some intervals sounding horribly out of tune.

The problem was eventually solved, or at least re-solved, during Bach's lifetime. A number of people figured out how to temper the scale in a relatively equal manner so that whatever key you chose to play in, it would be relatively in tune. To demonstrate this new method of tuning, Bach wrote two preludes and fugues for every key, and called the collection "Das Wohltemperierte Klavier", "The Well Tempered Keyboard". Well tempering was the first step towards the acceptance of equal tempering, in which every interval was tuned equally "well". Many musicians at that time disliked the relative out-of-tune-ness of every key that results in equal tempering, so it took a period of time for them to "evolve" into accepting it. The "Equal temperament" is now the standard tuning in every modern keyboard instrument.

The temperament, set into an octave in the middle of the keyboard, is the first thing that is done when a piano is tuned. After that, one string of every set of strings per note is tuned from the temperament octave. When I say "set", I am referring to the fact that in the mid-range and treble (top) of the piano there are three strings per note, in the tenor there are two, and in the bass there is just one. Finally, the other strings in the sets of strings, called "unisons", are tuned.

When I first started to tune, my Dad would do the first two steps, and then I would do the last. As I mastered this, he would move me onto the previous step. Each step is an art in itself, and it takes a lot of practice to do it well. There is also the matter of learning to become comfortable with the tuning tool, called a "hammer", not to mention the differences between pianos.

When a piano is tuned properly, it is actually put very accurately out-of-tune, because each interval is slightly compromised. It is no wonder, therefore, that my Dad used to call his trade, "The *Art* of Compromise".

Lt. Col. F.W. Musselwhite III
The author's grandfather,
with his tuning kit, circa 1930.

The Mechanics of Piano Tuning

To make money as a tuner, all the tools you really need could fit into your back pocket. This is one of the main advantages to learning how to tune a piano by ear. I can, and have, driven into a town in the middle of a longer journey, and within a few hours, made enough money for a meal and a hotel room. I didn't need a heavy tool kit, or a laptop computer or some other machine. All I needed was my ears, my skills, and the confidence to sell my services.

Of course, to repair or regulate takes a much larger tool kit, and a good deal more skills, but to just tune, all you need is a hammer, a tuning fork, a rubber mute, a Papp's mute, and a temperament strip.

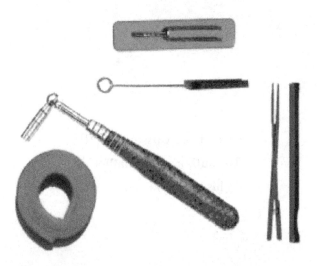

The Tuning Hammer

You need a professional quality tool to do a professional job. The tuning hammer normally stocked in your local music store is what is called in the trade, a student, or chipping hammer. Significantly cheaper than a professional hammer, it is lightweight, fixed in length, and does not have a removable tip. A professional hammer, available from a piano supply company, is heavier, balanced, can extend in length, and not only the tip, but the entire head can be removed. The handle is either made from nylon (as shown) or hardwood. Both the head and the tip come in different lengths.

The shorter the tip, the more the torque is transferred into the axis of the pin rather than the length. However, on some pianos, a short tip may not allow the handle to pass over the lid on upright pianos, or the plate struts on grands. The head can also come in different angles so that when the hammer is on the pin the handle rises either perpendicular to the piano or in varying degrees away from the piano. It is also important to be able to change the tip after it has worn too much to grab the pin adequately. The handle can extend, increasing leverage, making pins that are too tight in the block easier to turn.

Generally, the hammer is held at the very end when moving a pin; however, there are times when small adjustments can be made more accurately by grasping the handle closer to the head. When placing the hammer on the pin on an upright, align the handle so that it is more or less straight up and down. Grasp the end of the handle firmly, and hold your forearm so that it is level with the floor. Large movements are made with your entire arm, not just the forearm or wrist. Small adjustments, which will be covered later, are made in a slightly different manner using the wrist, with the forearm at the same angle as the handle.

Two important notes:

1. The tuning pin is basically a very fine-threaded screw. It can strip or wear out with too much torquing back and forth, and it can also bend, and even snap in half if bent enough.

2. On an upright piano, always hold on to the hammer when it is on a tuning pin. Do not leave the hammer on a pin as a placeholder if you leave the piano. If you are not holding the hammer, it should not be on a pin!

The Tuning Fork

The tuning fork is sounded in the following manner, and ONLY in the following manner:

Hold the very end of the fork with two fingers. Tap one tine onto your kneecap. With practice, you will find which part of the kneecap is the hardest and won't hurt. While the fork is ringing, you can listen to it either by holding it close to your ear, or hold the end against part of the piano, such as the cheek block (the blocks of wood at the ends of the keyboard) or the underside of the keybed.

One common trick is to hold the fork between the index and middle finger, press the end against the underside of the keybed, and then play the note to be tuned with the thumb of that same hand.

Do not hit it against a hard surface or drop it, as this will put the fork out of tune. When buying a fork, buy the most expensive, and therefore highest quality fork you can afford, but make sure that it is smaller than the palm of your hand with the fingers outstretched. You will need two: An "A" fork tuned to 440 cycles per second (cps), and a "C" fork tuned to 523.3 cps. If you get the opportunity, check your fork against a professional tuning machine for accuracy. It can be tuned if necessary by either lightly filing the inside ends of the tines to make it sharper, or the inside crotch of the tines to make it flatter.

NOTE: A tuning fork's accuracy is dependent on it being at room temperature. If cold, it will be sharp. If hot, it will be flat.

The Mutes

You need the following two kinds of mutes in your kit: A rubber mute with a metal handle, and a Papp's Mute.

As you know, each note in a piano may have more than one string. The mute is used for silencing one or two strings so that the strings can be tuned individually, without its unison ringing. It is inserted between the strings you want to silence. The closer to the striking point of the hammer, the more effective it will be.

The Papp's mute is a special mute used in tuning uprights. It is easier than a rubber mute to use when muting strings that are hidden behind the hammers. To insert it, you squeeze the handle gently, and either force it between two side-by-side unisons, or in the middle of three unisons to block the outside strings, or between the outside strings of two adjacent notes.

The Temperament Strip

This is a thick strip of felt, tapered narrower on one end. It is forced between the outside unison strings of two adjacent notes. The felt is inserted starting at the top of the middle section close to the Nut or Agraffe (the termination of the speaking length nearest the tuning pins), and looped over the top of the middle strings to let them ring. Continue looping until you either run out of strings or run out of felt. (I generally carry three strips - one for the treble section in a grand, one for the middle section and one for the bass.) When stripping the bass section, it mutes the left side of one pair, and the right side of the next.

The Mechanics of Tuning

The first step to becoming a good tuner is to master the mechanics of tuning: the use of the hammer, the way the pin reacts to being torqued or turned, and the way the string itself responds.

This, in itself, is probably the most important part of tuning, and the least understood and respected. It is of utmost importance that all tuners understand and master this skill whether they tune by ear or by machine. I have, on many occasions, rescued poor unsuspecting souls who have bought chipping hammers from the local music store thinking that they could tune their own piano. After trying to tune just a few notes, they have broken strings, bent pins, or complained that the pitch doesn't change when they turn the pin.

Here's a nice Canadian analogy to illustrate the process: When you go ice-skating, your skates must be tight in order for you to glide effortlessly and comfortably. You have to tighten the laces from the toe to the top, using a lacing hook to pull each loop as firmly as possible. Then the ends of the laces have to be wound around the upper ankle in the correct way, and tied with a special knot. To skip any of these steps means that your skates will quickly loosen, your ankles will be unsupported, and you'll fall on your face.

When tuning a piano, you have to keep in mind that any movement at the anchor end of the string will mean that the tuning will slip, so you should ensure first of all, that the string is tight to the plate. Then you have to be aware that as you turn the pin to tighten the string, the string may not follow through the agraffe, or over the nut and under the pressure bar at the same rate. Finally, the pin must actually turn in the block, and not just twist on itself.

When you loosen the string, the same forces are in effect, but in reverse. In addition to the above, each two plain string unisons are connected, so you have to make allowances for what effect tightening one side of the unison will have on the other. It is impossible to tune accurately without being aware of, and compensating for, these forces.

The following step-list, although referring to a single string, can be applied to every string. However, it is not the procedure used for pitch raising.

Step-by-Step Process of
Raising and Lowering the Pitch of a String

Ensure that the string is bedded firmly to the plate under the anchor pin. Using a brass rod shaped to a wedge, gently tap each side of the loop at the anchor pin, and tap the string lightly into the crotch of the pin.

(This should be done to all pins the first time you tune a particular piano. If you have done this step previously, or know that it has been done, then skip to the next step.)

Seat the string onto the bridge. Using the end of a hammer shank, tap or rub the string very lightly into the crotch of the bridge pins.

(If the piano is flat and needs a pitch-raise, only tap the string on the non-speaking side of the bridge. After the pitch has been raised, tap the speaking side.)

Make sure that the becket of the string (the bend at the pin) is firmly pushed into the tuning pin hole, and that the coil is tight together.

Put your finger on the key and then play the note. I know that this sounds insanely pedantic, but there are two ways to play a note when tuning: The Soft Blow, and The Hard Blow.

The soft blow is as hard as you can comfortably play the note without lifting your finger from the key.

The hard blow is raising your hand and playing it sharply with two fingers. The soft blow is not soft, however; musically speaking, a soft blow is between mezzo-forte to forte. A hard blow is at least fortissimo. It is important to consistently use the soft blow while tuning, or else the next good player who comes along will put it out of tune with one fortissimo chord.

Change the pitch of the string by gently turning the pin in small nudges. Do not just listen for the sound of the note changing; you must **feel the pin turn** in the pinblock.

If the string was flat in pitch, raise it slightly higher than the desired pitch, release the handle and listen again. It should still be slightly sharp. Give the key a hard blow and listen again. If it is still flat, turn the pin a little more. **It is very important to not over-turn the pin!** Not only will you prematurely loosen the pin, but you will lose stability, not to mention waste time.

Unless the piano has oversized pins, there should be a little play between the tuning hammer tip and the pin. Use this play to gently tap the pin laterally by raising the handle of the hammer while the tip is on the pin and gently tapping the handle down. **Do not bend the pin in any way!**

With new tips, it is sometimes necessary to back the tip a little off of the pin to create a slack space between the tip and the pin. Tapping inside of the slack space is your way of seeing if the string is frozen against the contact points between the speaking length and the tuning pin. This takes a lot of practice, but after a while it becomes an automatic motion.

If the string was sharp, first use the slack-tip tap method to see where the hidden tension of the string is. It might just tap onto pitch. If it doesn't, nudge the pin so that the pitch lowers to just above the desired pitch, play the note with a hard blow and listen again. If it is still sharp, nudge it again. If it is on pitch, slack-tip tap to see if it goes flat. If it does, slack-tip tap upwards, to see if it raises. If it does, leave it on pitch. If it is still flat, nudge the pitch up.

If you encounter a tuning pin that is too loose to adequately hold pitch, mark the tip of the pin with chalk, and test the rest of the pins before you carry on with tuning. The loose pins can then be replaced as a group.

(**NOTE:** *If you notice a number of loose pins in a row or in a cluster, it may indicate a cracked or de-laminated pinblock*).

Conversely, if you encounter pins that are so tight that they "snap" when turning (not literally break, but move with a snapping motion), move the handle of the tuning hammer close to a portion of the piano's case or plate and brace your hand against it when turning the hammer. In this case, the nudging motion does not work. Instead, try to carefully raise the pitch of the string, and then hard blow and tap to set the pin.

The combination of soft blow, hard blow, nudging and tapping, will not only result in a more stable tuning, but it will also save time and energy once it becomes second nature. To simply pull the string up to pitch or to push it down, will not only waste your time, but it is hard on the piano, your body, and your customer's ears. A sure sign of an inexperienced tuner is the sound of a string being raised and lowered over and over.

Hammer Technique 101

Tools Needed For This Section:

1. Short tip Extendable Tuning Hammer
2. Three Rubber Mutes
2. One temperament Strip
3. Two Tuning Forks: A:440 & C:523.3.

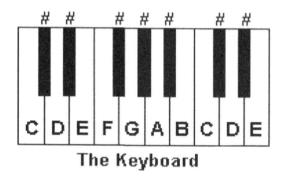

The Keyboard

Exercise #1

Start by inserting rubber mutes so that they block out the right-hand two unisons of A below middle C, the E above middle C, and the A above middle C. Play the fork by hitting it on the knee cap. Play the A above middle C, place the hammer on the pin for the speaking string and try to match that note to the fork.

There are two ways to do this:

You can play the fork, holding the end of the fork between the index and middle fingers of one hand, and then play the note with your thumb and hold the end of the fork against the bottom of the keybed, underneath the note you are holding.

If you are brave, stick the end of the fork between your teeth.

Play the fork, and the A, and listen for a warble or vibrato called "beats".

Remember how fast the beats are, and tune the A below so that it beats the same speed. Then check that note against the fork and tune the A above to the A below.

For the sake of this exercise, just play the note, compare it to the fork, and then tune the string to where you think it will match. Play the fork again and repeat it till the note and the fork are beatless together. When you have done this you can congratulate yourself on completing the first step to learning how to tune.

Give yourself as long as you need to do this step accurately, and then try to do the same thing using the tuning fork in the different ways explained previously.

Remember that Rome wasn't built in a day. Go

slowly, and give yourself plenty of time to master each new section in this book.

Exercise #2

Tune the A above Middle C so that it is beatless with the fork. Now tune the A an octave below so that it is beatless with the A above. Next, tune the E above middle C to the A below so that it is beatless.

Now play the E and the A above at the same time and listen for the beats. Play the E and the A below and compare it to the upper combination of notes.

Notice how the upper two notes beat fast when played together while the lower two are beatless. Now tune the E so that it is beatless with the A above. Try the lower A and the E and listen to the speed of the beats. Now the lower beats fast and the upper is pure.

Now tune the E so that it beats with both the upper A and the lower A at the same rate. Practice matching the beat rates until you can manipulate the pin so that you can make these very minute adjustments.

Exercise #3

Once you have the "feel" of the tuning hammer, check the upper A to make sure that it is beatless to the fork. Tune the E below so that it beats about once per second with the A above, and then tune the A below middle C so that it is beatless with the E. Now, check the A to A octave. Bring the lower A just a little sharper so that you just begin to hear the beat between the two A's slow down to almost nothing. Check the Lower A with the E above and balance the A below so that there is a slightly noticeable beat with the E but practically no beat with the A above.

Finally, check the lower A against the fork. If you have done the above exercise properly, the upper A will be completely beatless with the fork, but the lower A, while not really beating, is not perfectly pure, either.

If this works, then congratulations! You now have not only learned how to manipulate the pin with proper hammer technique, but you have also tempered two notes: the lower A and the E.

It would be best if you could find an established tuner to be a mentor, for there is nothing better than having the instant feedback to correct your mistakes before they become ingrained.

In addition, probably the best way to learn

would be to start with mastering tuning the unisons and the octaves, before tackling the temperament. However, unless you have a temperament set into the piano, practicing the unisons and octaves are nothing more than practicing the mechanics. It is the most important skill to learn, so continue on once you think you have "the feel" of how to set the pin properly, and can do the above exercises fairly effortlessly.

C.H. Musselwhite, Piano Technician.

The Temperament

"Beauty is in the eye of the beholder". The fact of the matter is, when a piano is considered beautifully "in tune", it is actually out of tune in a very precise manner.

To a trained singer, violinist, or for that matter any instrumentalist who does not use a keyboard of some type, this "out-of-tune-ness" is not only obvious to them, but they have to learn to accept it as the "standard sound" of a tuned piano.

At the other extreme, people learn to accept the sound of an un-tuned, or poorly tuned piano as well.

As a professional piano tuner, it is part of our job to not only tune well, but to teach our customers the importance of having their piano properly tuned, and keeping it in tune.

Over the past four centuries, a lot of very brilliant musical minds have given us not only the amazing instrument/machine/art called a piano, but have established what the sound of the piano should be. If we are charged with preserving their legacies, it behooves us to take this task seriously and professionally, and master this "Art of Compromise".

It is interesting to note that to the player, the most noticeable (and therefore the most important) parts of the tuning are, in order: the unisons; then the octaves; and finally, the temperament.

The layman will instantly recognize when a unison is out of tune, but rarely notice when the temperament is poorly set. To the tuner, however, the opposite is the case: The temperament is of utmost importance; then the octaves (and the stretch); then, last but not least, the unisons.

As explained in the introduction, the temperament is an attempt to squeeze twelve semitones plus the Pythagorean comma into the space of twelve steps: thirteen into twelve.

It is as if we were building a staircase twelve feet high, but were instructed to use thirteen risers. Each step, therefore, would be 9.23076" high instead of ten inches. However, even after carefully measuring and cutting, when assembled, we find that the staircase is still a fraction of an inch too high. To correct this, we either have to shorten one or two steps to make it fit, or carefully shorten each step by an infinitesimal but equal amount. Historical (unequal) temperaments are like the first solution, while the equal temperament is like the latter.

Each semitone has to be made slightly smaller than a perfect semitone in order for twelve semitones to equal an octave.

Unlike the staircase example, the Pythagorean comma is not a full step. In technical terms, the difference between semi-tones is measured in units known as cents. We say that an increase of a semitone in pitch on the piano keyboard equals 100 cents. However, a pure semitone, mathematically, is exactly 101.95 cents. Therefore, the extra "step" that we have to squeeze into the twelve steps of the scale is 23.5 cents, or a little less than a quartertone. *(It's actually 23.46 cents, but I've rounded everything up.)* Each note we tune has to be 1.95 cents off of perfect to compensate for the extra 23.5 cents that has to be included in the octave.

In order to properly explain the techniques involved in setting the temperament, a little clarification of terminology is necessary: First of all, the names of the keys.

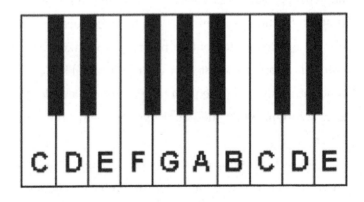

The black notes above the white notes are named "sharp" (#) e.g. the black note above the note C is C Sharp (C#). Musically speaking, the black notes below the white notes are named "flat" (b). However, a black note is only referred to as "flat" in the context of music. A semitone (the musical step between one key to the next whether black or white) is referred to in music as a minor second or "m2". Two semitones, or a whole tone, is a Major second or "M2". Note that the "M" is capitalized when Major. (Please refer to the chart on the next page.)

The Keyboard Intervals

Starting at the top left corner and going down, you see the intervals in chromatic order. If you look across the top row, you will see an example of the sequence of Major thirds used in The Augmented Chord Check discussed on p.25. As you can see, the naming of the intervals is not completely straightforward. Some intervals, the fourth, fifth and octave, are called Perfect (even though on the piano they are not), and what would logically be called a minor fifth is referred to as a diminished fifth. The reason for these terms stem from their use in music, but what is important is that you memorize the names of these intervals and learn to recognize their sound.

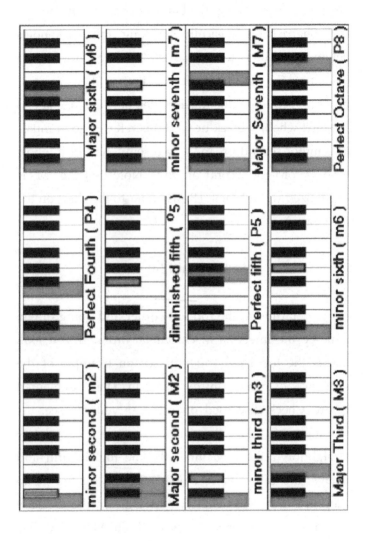

Many music students use a little trick to learn the sound of intervals – they associate an interval with a song.

For example: The first two notes in "My Bonnie Lies Over The Ocean" are a Major sixth. The first two notes of the theme from "Love Story" are a minor sixth. It is important to note that the "Perfect" intervals, the fourth, fifth and octave, are beatless when they are "perfect"ly in tune with each other, or what tuners would describe as "Pure" intervals. When we temper the tuning of the piano, we alter these pure intervals in order to include the Pythagorean Comma.

For example, let's use two notes on the keyboard: The F below middle C and the G below middle C. To compensate for the comma, we need to bring these two notes closer together by 3.9 cents. If we tune the C above these two notes to a tuning fork, we can use this note as a reference. From this C down to the F is a Perfect fifth (P5). From the C down to the F is a Perfect fourth (P4). The sound of a pure perfect fifth is rather ingrained into the ears of western civilization. From the drone of a bagpipe, to the chanting of a medieval chorus, our ears "know" the sound of a pure fifth, so we strive to make this interval as clean as possible, while still less than perfect.

The sound of a perfect fourth is less ingrained,

but still recognizable, so we can alter the interval more than we can alter the fifth without making musically trained ears uncomfortable.

3.9 cents less than perfect, however, is still a big enough difference as to be easily recognized by the trained ear. So, we compensate by making the fifth slightly smaller, and the fourth slightly bigger. If we made both smaller, it would cancel the comma, and if we made both bigger it would increase the comma.

To keep the fifth sounding pure-ish, we give it less error than we do the fourth. Tuners use the term "Narrow" to describe an interval made smaller or closer together, and the term "Wide" to describe an Interval made bigger or farther apart.

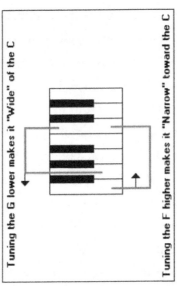

Although there are many ways to set the temperament, we will start with a series of intervals known as the "Circle of Fourths and Fifths". This pattern is sometimes referred to as "Chasing the Tail".

An Important Note About Time: *It is not unusual for beginning tuners to spend hours trying to tune a piano. This is a very difficult and frustrating process for most people, and many give up and use an electronic tuner to bypass the agony of learning. Don't despair, be patient with yourself!*

The two keys to learning anything new are:

1. **Interest**. If you have the interest, you have the motivation, which is the most important thing you need.
2. **Simplification**. Anything can be broken up into smaller bits, and smaller bits are easier to grasp.

In the initial learning stage, don't worry about tuning the whole piano. Concentrate on tuning ONE string, then ONE unison set, then ONE octave, etc.

Your goal is to eventually be able to tune a piano within about an hour. In order to do that, you have to master the steps along the way and become faster at each step. This is the main way to increase speed. With practice you should be able to set the temperament within ten minutes or so. That's it! Don't worry about any other part of the tuning as a whole. Setting the temperament is only about 10% of the total task, so strive toward doing an "okay" job within about ten minutes time.

Remember: *The customer will be more concerned about how well your unisons are set. As you become better at all the skills, your quality will improve automatically. Don't let yourself fall into the trap of striving for perfection first. Instead, strive for efficiency.*

I am often asked how I tune a piano so quickly. The secret is threefold.

First: Skill with the hammer acquired over time.

Second: The ability to hear quickly when something is right, and not second-guess yourself. (As my Dad often said: "If it's not broke, don't fix it!").

Thirdly: (And this is where the majority of tuners are challenged), **Don't Waste Time**. Don't check if it's not necessary, and don't waste time fiddling around, playing unnecessary runs, trills or catchy little ditties. Save your playing of the piano until the end, when it will seem like a reward for finishing.

Playing a lot during the tuning can seem to a listener like vanity and procrastination, while being efficient with the process will make the customer feel that you are truly a professional.

temperament Pattern #1 - "Chasing the Tail"

First, insert a temperament strip between the unison sets of each note so that it mutes the outside strings of each set from at least the E below middle C to the G above middle C.

NOTE: Always press down the damper pedal when inserting the strip. The action of inserting the strip can move the strings together, which could damage the damper felt.

Start by tuning the middle C to a tuning fork tuned to C: 523.3 beats per minute (bpm.). Compare the fork to the C above middle C and listen to the speed of the beats between the note on the piano and the fork. Determine if it is sharp or flat of the fork.

Now, tune the middle C so that it beats to the C above at the same rate. Next, check the middle C with your fork. If it is beatless, then you have successfully tuned that note. Listen to the note for at least four or five seconds. If middle C beats against the fork, then you misjudged the direction (sharp or flat) that you altered middle C.

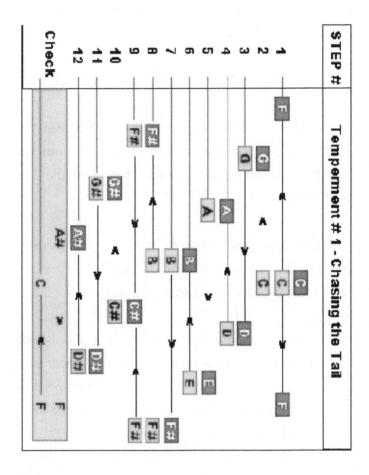

STEP 1: Once middle C is in tune, play it and the F below middle C at the same time.

(Remember that although this interval is called a perfect fifth, to temper the F it must be sharp of perfect or "narrow".)

Bring the note so that it is absolutely beatless, and then raise it sharp to the point where it just starts to beat. Somewhere between beatless and beating is a spot where the beats are described as "just rolling over". It is so slow as to be imperceptible unless you listen to these two notes for three or more seconds.

Now, tune the F above middle C, using the F an octave below. Every time you tune an octave, keep in mind that you are stretch tuning, and the octaves are not exactly pure.

This particular octave, called the temperament Octave, is the purest in the whole piano, but still the goal is to make the upper F sharper than the lower F WITHOUT HEARING A BEAT. I know this sounds impossible on paper, but in practice, you will soon find that there is a very small range of play to the octaves where it can be slightly under or over without hearing any beats.

Test the upper F to the middle C, and make sure that it beats at least as fast as your heartbeat. (Check your pulse on the carotid artery of your neck as a reference.) If you can't make the C-F P4 beat, then either your FF P8 is too pure or narrow, or your F-C P5 is too slow.

STEP 2: Now, tune the G below middle C to the C. This "Perfect Fourth" should beat exactly the same as the C F P4. An important point to note here is that the slower your fifths are, the faster your fourths will have to be.

STEP 3: Tune the D above middle C to the G you just tuned, keeping the fifth narrow.

STEP 4: Tune the A a fourth down from the D. It is at this point that you will be able to check if your fifths and fourths are beating at the right rate. Play the F-C P5 and listen for the slow rollover. Now play the D-G P5 and compare the speed of the rollover to the first P5.

It is very important to take your time here; there is a time and place for speed and THIS IS NOT IT!

Now check the speed of the C-G P4 to the D-A P4. Their beat rates must match exactly. Finally, play the F-A M3. It should beat around 6-7 bps, or about as fast as you can *easily* say wah-wah-wah-wah-wah-wah-wah. If it is beating too slowly, then either your fourths are beating too fast, or your fifths are too pure. Check your fourths and fifths again. If you're certain that they are right, then **continue on to the next step**.

NOTE: There is a natural tendency to try to make the fourths too pure. Keep in mind that it is possible to tune the fifths perfect, and the fourths quite fast, and still end up making everything basically equal. This kind of temperament results in a huge stretch and is often used by concert tuners to make a piano sound brighter and more exciting in a large reverberant place such as a cathedral.

Doing the opposite, tuning the fifths and fourths beating equally, gives you a less lively-sounding piano. This "blended" temperament is the type of temperament found in electronic keyboards, and although acceptable, it is important that you know the sound of narrow fifths and wide fourths before the more advanced temperaments are explained. Without almost pure fifths, it is difficult to adequately do the stretch tuning covered later.

Now we continue this pattern of fourths and fifths until we end up back at middle C.

STEP 5: Tune the E from the A below.

STEP 6: Tune the B from the A.

STEP 7: Next, tune the F# above middle C from the B below.

STEP 8: Tune the F# an octave below. Make sure that when tuning this octave, that you tune the lower F# so that it is slightly wide and beats properly with the B a P4 above.

STEP 9: Tune the C# to the lower F#, checking it with the upper F# P4.

STEP 10: Tune the G# a P4 below the C#.

STEP 11: Tune the D# to the G#.

STEP 12: Tune A# to the D# P4.

Stop there! Don't check the A#-F P5, but rather go back to the beginning and make sure that every fourth and fifth are beating properly. Play the F-C P5, and then go up in semitones very slowly (F#-C#, G-D, G#-D#, etc.). They should all have the same beat rate. Now do the same thing with the P4's (F-A#, F#-B, etc.) You should be able to check them by playing each succeeding interval after a little more than a second for each chord. In other words, you should hear the beat a second after playing the interval, move up, hear the next beat, and so on. They must have the same beat rate. If they don't, you have to start again and fix any mistakes you might have made along the way.

Now we get to the interesting part: Play the F

above middle C and the P5 down to the A#. If it doesn't beat the same as the other fifths, then memorize how fast the interval is beating, and figure out if the A# is sharp or flat by tapping up or down. If all the P5's and P4's are beating at the right rate, and constant in speed from one P4 to the next, etc., then you can figure out quite easily where you went wrong in your "Staircase-Building Compromise".

If the A# is sharp of where it should be, your P4's are beating too slowly. If the A# is flat or not beating at all, your P4's are beating too fast. Play the P4's and take a good guess as to how fast they should be beating, in order to go through the whole thing again and end up at the right place.

Here's a little hint: You'll probably be way off! This temperament pattern, because it goes in a circle back to the beginning, makes it very easy to multiply small mistakes into a bad finishing interval.

The only way to prevent this happening is to test your progress along the way by using what tuners refer to as "checks".

Play the F below middle C and the A above it. This M3 should be beating about 6-7 beats per second (bps.) If the A#-F P5 is beating about this fast, the amount you will have to change each P4 amounts to about less than .5 bps. This is such a small amount that you probably won't be able to change all the P4's to compensate for that amount, without getting clues to "check" your progress along the way.

temperament Pattern #2 - "Beating around the Bush"

Here is a slight alternative to "Chasing the Tail" that incorporates quite a few handy checks. I call it "Beating around the Bush".

It starts exactly like the pattern explained in the previous section. Do the pattern again starting with the heading labeled, "temperament Pattern #1". When you reach the place where it says: "**continue on to the next step**", continue on below.

STEP 5: At this point, we have tuned Middle C, F below, G below, A below D above, and the F above.

Tune the C# above middle C so that the A-C# M3 is faster than the F-A M3, and the C#-F M3 is faster still. Think of the C# as being halfway between the A and the F, but a little closer to the A.

(We'll get back to this note again later in this temperament pattern, but it's good to have it close to use as a reference.)

When you believe that the C# sounds right, then tune the F# a P5 below, and the F# a P4 above.

Remember to get the beat rates right, and tune the octave a hair narrow. You shouldn't exactly hear any beating, but it still can't be a perfect "Perfect Octave".

STEP 6: Tune the B between the two F#'s.

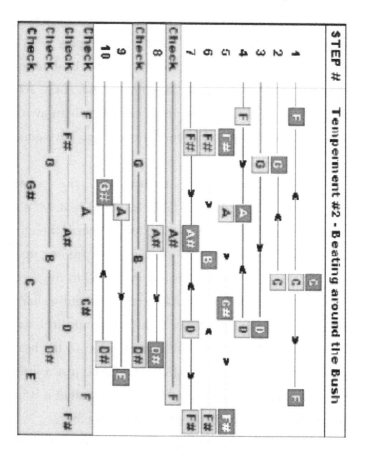

STEP 7: Tune the A# so that it beats with the F# M3 below just a shade faster than the F-A M3.

If everything has gone well, you now have one of the most useful checks available to you: The Augmented Chord Check.

Play the following series of two-note M3 chords: F-A, then A-C#, then C#-F. Each M3 should beat slightly faster than the one before it. Now play F#-A#, A#-D, then D-F#. Again, each M3 should beat faster than the one before it. Now play F-A, F#-A#, A-C#, A#-D, C#-F, and D-F#. This sequence can tell you an awful lot about where you have gone wrong, if you have gone wrong at all.

As always, the farther up the scale chromatically a third is, the faster it should beat. M3's a semitone apart should be quite close in speed, though, enough for you to see if they are indeed speeding up.

Now check the A# below middle C to the P5 F above. Remember that the A# should be slightly sharp of perfect, making a narrow fifth that should just roll over slowly. Play the A#-D M3, and listen to the beat rate. Now, play the A-C# M3. It should be just a little slower. If it's not, then tune the C# again so that it is in the middle beat-wise between the A and the F.

Now, when you play the following sequence, each third should beat faster than the third below: F-A

M3, A-C# M3, and C#-F M3.

Now, try the A-C# M3 and the A#-D M3. The higher a third is chromatically, the faster it should beat. If this does not happen, check all the fifths you have tuned to make sure they sound the same. Then, check the fourths.

The most common cause for things not working out in this pattern is having one or two of the notes beating in the wrong direction; i.e. the A in the A-D P4 tuned narrow instead of wide. Remember: The fifths are narrow and the fourths are wide. **A narrow fourth can still have the same beat rate as a wide fourth.**

STEP 8: With all the checks explained previously, we should be pretty certain that the A# is right. Use it to tune the D# a P4 above. We can now use the Augmented Chord Check on that D#. Play the GB M3, then the B-D# M3. If the upper third is faster, then continue on.

STEP 9: Tune the E above middle C using the A a P5 below, the B a P4 below, and check it with the C an M3 below. With so many notes to check it to, it should be fairly clear where it should be.

STEP 10: Tune the G# below middle C using the D#

above, or the C#. (Or, for that matter, any other note you want.)

If you have done everything properly, they're all in tune! Congratulations, you can now use the Augmented Check on all the notes in the temperament.

temperament Pattern #3 – Diefenbaugh

Now that you have explored the two rudimentary temperament patterns (and hopefully have the sound of the escalating thirds planted firmly in your mind), we'll explore the concept of temperaments at a slightly more advanced level, and look at using thirds as tuning intervals rather than as just checks.

This pattern is called the "Diefenbaugh" because it was named after its biggest proponent and probable inventor, George Diefenbaugh, the former head of the Service Department for Kawai USA Inc.

The first big difference is that we'll use an A: 440 fork, rather than the C. Tune the A above middle C so that it precisely matches the fork, and then tune the A below middle C so it is on the wide side of beatless.

STEP 1: Tune the F below middle C to the lower A so that it does the normal 6-7 bps (wah-wah, etc.).

STEP 2: Tune the F above middle C to the F below. (Fifths narrow, fourths wide!)

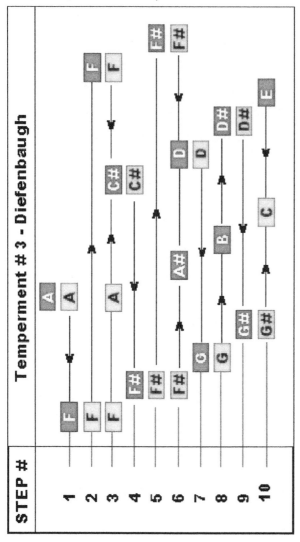

STEP 3: Tune the C# so that it beats slightly faster to the F than it does to the A. You can now do the Augmented Check F-A, A-C#, C#-F. Make sure that each third gets faster as you play the higher chord.

STEP 4: Tune the F# below middle C to the C#.

STEP 5: Tune the F# above to the F# below.

STEP 6: Using the F#'s, tune the A# and the D. You now have many other checks you can do to test these two notes.

STEP 7: Now tune the G below middle C to the D.

STEP 8: Using thirds, tune the B and the D#. There are a lot of tests you can do here, as well.

STEP 9: Tune the G# below middle C using thirds (or any other applicable interval - there are quite a few.)

STEP 10: Tune the E above middle C. Remember that you started with an A fork, so it should be VERY obvious if you have done this temperament pattern properly.

temperament Pattern #4 - Thirds and Fifths

Just in case you wanted another option similar to the Diefenbaugh, here is a temperament pattern only using thirds and fifths. (Of course, you can always use fourths as checks along the way).

I use this pattern when I am pitch raising, or if I'm in a big hurry. With practice it can give you a decent-sounding temperament very quickly - if you're not too fussy about what the fourths sound like!

As I mentioned earlier, it is very important when you are just learning to tune the temperament that you don't rush. The standard principle to learning anything new is two steps forward, and one step back. Push yourself towards speed and efficiency, but don't skip steps, and don't rush.

New tuners often spend an hour or more putting a good temperament down, but it is with time and practice that speed and accuracy comes, not by rushing the learning process. With practice, you will eventually be able to lay a good temperament in less than ten minutes, but don't be frustrated with how long a tuning is taking. With practice and patience, your speed will increase and your accuracy will improve.

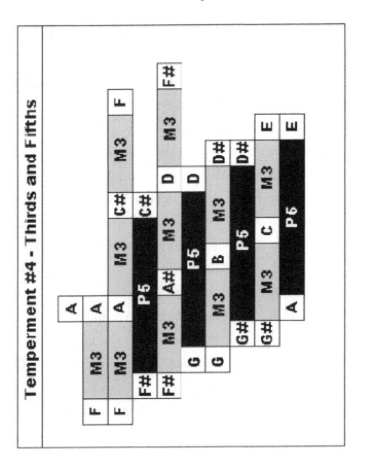

temperament Pattern # 5
The "Blended" temperament.

I rarely use this style of temperament, but it has its uses. It is most similar to the type of tempering found in electronic keyboards, and many of the electronic tuners that I have tested.

It results in fourths and fifths that are fairly close in speed, which makes a satisfying stretch difficult to lay down, and gives the piano a less exciting sound. However, it has one huge benefit: Using this concept, thirds and sixths have roughly the same beat speed, which means that you have more checks available, and these checks are very easy to hear.

The basic concept here is that even though the fifths are narrow and the fourths wide, they are basically the same speed: a slightly faster roll-over than we normally put in the fifths is also used in the fourths. It is too slow to count accurately, but it is noticeable when the fourths are too fast compared to each other.

The pattern starts like the thirds and fifths pattern explained previously. The trick here is to make sure that you are compromising EVERY interval but the octave. In other words, no interval will be even close to beatless (except the octave).

The best thing about this temperament is that

the M3 and the M6 above any given note will have the same beat rate and will progress evenly as they rise chromatically in pitch. If you know what you are listening for, it doesn't matter which pattern you use.

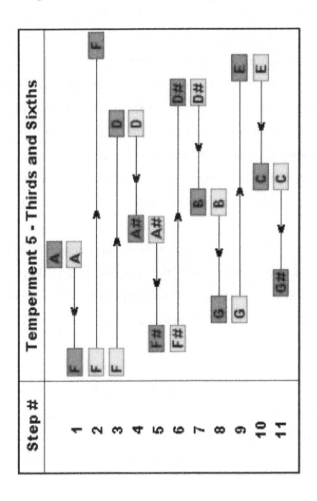

temperament Pattern #6 - The 6-3-3

Every pattern is just a tool to help you hear how you are tempering each note. This pattern is one of my favourites. Not only does it work well and sound nice, but it also has a lot of checks built in, and is very easy to remember when you are starting out.

After setting the A and the two F's, you tune a sixth up and then two thirds down. Then, another sixth up, and two thirds down – hence, the nickname, "The 6-3-3".

The other interesting part of this pattern is that every interval is tuned wide.

STEPS 1&2: First, set the A to your fork, then tune the F an M3 down (6-7 bps -wah-wah, etc.), then the A below middle C so that it is wide, and then the F a P8 above.

This is where the fun really starts.

STEP 3: Tune the D a P6 up from the F sharp, so that it beats exactly the same speed as the F-A M3. (Technically, the interval of the sixth should beat a tiny bit faster, but it is easier while you are still learning if you match the beat rate.)

STEP 4: Tune the A# a P3 down from the D so that it beats a little faster than the F-A M3. You can then check the A# against the two F's on either side to make sure that they beat roughly the same.

(Because of scaling differences in some pianos, you may have to make the P4's beat slightly faster than the P5's, but you don't have to be too picky at this point.)

STEP 5: Tune the F# an M3 below the A# you just tuned so that it beats slightly faster than the F-A M3, but slower than the A#-D M3. At this point it will be obvious if your A# is not right.

STEP 6: Tune the D# a P6 up from the F# so that it beats the same speed as the F#-A# M3.

STEP 7: Tune the B an M3 down from the D# you just tuned, so that it beats slightly faster than the A#-D M3.

STEP 8: Tune the G an M3 down from the B. You can now do the Augmented Chord Check covered previously in this chapter. You can also check this G to the P5 - D above.

STEP 9: Tune the E a P6 up so that it beats the same speed as the G-B M3.

STEP 10: Tune the C an M3 down from the E.

STEP 11: Tune the G# an M3 down from the C. To use this pattern to make a normal stretch temperament, make the sixths beat about 7-8 bps compared to the M3's 6-7 bps. Temper the octaves slightly wide, and when you check the fourths and fifths, make the fifths as clean as possible.

Troubleshooting your Temperament

Everyone struggles with the temperament. Even seasoned tuners can have an "off" day, or encounter a piano that seems to fight the process from beginning to end. However, a couple of quick pointers can save you some grief.

Many small pianos have extremely compromised scaling which can cause problems in tuning. If you have to tune a piano where the trichords start in the middle of the temperament octave, you can be sure that setting the initial notes are going to be tricky. One way to solve this is to set the temperament in a higher register; however, this takes some practice.

Another simpler way is to take your best guess, and then duplicate the temperament an octave up.

Mute the whole mid-section, tune the temperament, and then tune the G-G P8, the G#-G# P8, etc. As you tune, check the fourths and fifths as you go.

If you have made an error lower down, it will multiply itself higher up, making it easier to spot and to fix. Just fix the error up high, and then transfer the fix to the lower octave.

The same solutions can be applied if you have trouble setting the temperament in any given piano. Just tune the temperament over two octaves and make note of where the error reproduces itself.

For instance: Say the problem stems from you making the E above middle C slightly flat. As soon as you tune the A below middle C to the A above, the fourth will be beating way too fast. Simply lower the E, and suddenly, the E-A P4 is beating at the right speed.

As I have said earlier, if your temperament isn't perfect, chances are that most people won't hear the problem. This isn't to say that you can do a sloppy job every time; instead, it means that you can relax about trying to be perfect, and just do the best job you can with the time that you have. The next time you tune, you will do better. Practice does make perfect.

The most common error in setting the

temperament is having an interval beat at the right speed but tuned in the wrong direction.

If you set the interval perfect first, and then make it narrow or wide, you will avoid this problem. If you get to the end and things don't work out, first check the beat rates by comparing an ascending series of perfect fifths, i.e.: F-C P5, F#-C# P5, G-D P5, etc. Or perfect fourths, or Major thirds, or Major sixths. (Practice playing these series of intervals until you can do them smoothly and confidently.)

If you don't hear a problem, then check the direction of the interval spread by going through the temperament pattern again, and slack-tip tap each note lightly to test which way they are tuned.

Problem Solving

Sometimes it can seem as if the entire career of tuning is an exercise in problem solving, but to many people, problem solving is the spice of life.

Setting the temperament is a lot like doing a crossword puzzle - a pleasurable pastime rather than a chore. Every clue you get, gives you a clue toward the solution. If you pay attention, you will soon notice that one mistake you made early in the pattern has affected something later on; an interval near the end; a slow third in the middle of the ascending Major third check; an octave that doesn't work with a P5. Instead of ignoring the signs, check back and see where you might have gone wrong. Think of it as doing the crossword in pencil, and erasing a wrong answer. As soon as you take away the wrong one, sometimes the right one presents itself!

The Octaves

Tuning the octaves is much more than playing an octave above and tuning two notes together. Each octave away from the temperament is tempered itself, not only to achieve a "stretch" tuning, but also to align the note each note you are tuning to the harmonic sequence inherent in each individual note.

The Harmonic Sequence

Re-read this quote from the introduction to this book:

"If you play a string, and then divide it in half by placing your finger on the middle of the string (what physicists call "the node"), you would hear a note one octave higher than the first note, which is called the 'Fundamental'. (If you play middle C on a piano, and the C above it that is in tune, that is an octave.)

If you then divide that half in half again, you would hear a 'Perfect Fifth' above the Octave. (Like playing C and the G above it.) If you continued to subdivide the string in this manner, you would hear a rather mysterious thing: a note two octaves higher, then a third (C to E) above that, then the fifth, then a minor 7th (C to A#), then all the diatonic notes (like all the white keys), and then every single note.

If you could go even further, you would hear microtones, which are not part of the western scale, but which are a part of the music of other cultures."

You can experiment with this in real life. You need a grand piano, preferably one that is in tune.

Play the C, two octaves below middle C, and check the tuning of that note against the octave above. Hopefully it will be a reasonably pure octave. Now, find the middle of that string while it vibrates, and hold your finger lightly against the string. Now play it repeatedly while you move the position of your finger up and down the string until you clearly hear the first harmonic (the C an octave above the note you are playing). Check the tuning of that harmonic against the octave. You should be able to hear a slight difference in the beat rate.

Now, check against two octaves above, and

three octaves, etc. Each octave will have a different beat rate. If you take the time to tune all those octaves pure, and then re-tune them to match the harmonic you'll notice that the harmonic is definitely sharp of the fundamental - the note you are playing, rather than the harmonic.

The spot where you are touching the string is called the first node. If you move your finger closer toward you on the string, you will find the other higher nodes. If you test the tuning of these harmonics, you will find that they are even sharper than the first.

The reason why there are not as many dampers as there are strings, is so that the upper strings will ring sympathetically with the lower strings. However, these strings will only vibrate if they are excited by another vibration in the same pitch harmonically. Therefore, in order to set the upper strings ringing, they have to line up tuning-wise with the harmonics of the lower strings.

The only way to do that is to tune them sharp. They won't ring with the fundamentals of the lower notes because their own fundamentals start too high.

The sound of a piano is greatly affected by the acoustics of the room, and the ability of the soundboard to reproduce the sounds of the strings. If a piano is in a small dead room, the effect of a high stretch can be too apparent in the octaves. In a large reverberant room, you can stretch the octaves to a truly ridiculous point before it will become apparent to a listener at the other end of the room. The big stretch in the big room will excite the upper strings and make the piano stand out. However, a big stretch in a small room may make the upper strings resonate, but it will also make the stretched octaves annoying to the listener.

Therein lies another part of the Art of Compromise, and another reason why aural tuning is superior: Every piano has to be tuned differently - and tuned differently in every space - in order for it to sound its best. There is no magic formula for determining how much to stretch the octaves. The only way to correctly determine it is to let the piano tell you, and for you to hear it.

To Strip or Not to Strip

I strip every note on the piano in a grand, and everything except the treble in an upright. It is because, in essence, what I am doing in the stretch is extending the temperament to each end of the keyboard. It is easier to do the same kinds of checks as in the temperament octave higher up, or lower down, if you don't have to worry about your unisons while you tune the octaves.

Personally, I don't see any reason why not to do this. It's not as if not stripping saves time; the time you save not inserting the strip will probably be small, compared to the time you waste getting the octaves and unisons to line up properly with the temperament octave.

There is another reason to strip:

If, when the strip is in, you still hear the muted unisons because they are so far out of tune, then you know instantly that the piano needs a pitch raise.

Back when I used a rubber mute to tune past the temperament, I would sometimes get halfway through the treble or bass before I realized that that section of the piano was so flat as to not be stable. It was a bit of an embarrassing situation to inform the customer at that point in the process that my fee had suddenly gone up.

If you strip first, set the pitch of the piano, and quickly play the keyboard chromatically, it will be very apparent if the piano needs a pitch raise.

When you strip the bass section, make note of the pattern that you have to make in skipping from pin to pin with the hammer. It is always symmetrical, so you don't have to waste time figuring out where to put your hammer for the next string.

There will be an easily followed pattern if you

look for it. Often the muted strings are the "inside" pins in a set of four. In some pianos, the ringing strings go: Left up, right down, skip two, etc. After you have some experience under your belt in recognizing all these patterns, tuning a stripped bass is no more difficult then tuning a stripped treble.

Order of Tuning

There is a specific order that the octaves should be tuned so that you balance the change of stress over the entire scale.

First, tune upwards until you are one octave into the top section. (If you tune past this point, the chances are great that you will have to retune the upper octaves once you have finished the bass section.)

As a whole, the wound strings are under greater tension than either section of plain strings. Additionally, the shorter the string, the less movement is needed to change its pitch. Therefore, as you tune the lower sections you add or subtract stress to the piano. In some pianos, this can cause a large enough movement to alter the pitch of the higher, shorter strings. This is because the strings press down on the soundboard, which is convex. As you raise the pitch of the strings, you increase the amount of downward pressure on the soundboard.

After you have finished the first octave of the top section, tune downwards into the bass until you reach the lowest note. After that, the temperament strip is pulled out note by note until the top of the middle section.

Before continuing to tune the unisons further, the octaves in the top section should be checked for a change in pitch.

The Stretch

Here are two quick little exercises to illustrate the concept of stretch tuning:

Start with a piano that is tune. Strip the mid-section of the piano, and tune the C an octave below middle C so that it is beatless to your fork. Now, tune the G a P5 above the lower C so that it is pure. Tune the D a P5 up from the G so that it is pure, and finally, tune the A a P5 up from the D also pure. Now compare the A against your A tuning fork. You should notice that it beats about 4 bps. That is the difference between pure octaves, and tempered octaves.

For the next exercise it is best to have a grand piano at your disposal.

Play the second lowest A on the keyboard and

subdivide the string with your finger so that it rings the second harmonic - the E below middle C. Play the key hard so that the harmonic is very strong and at the same time, play the E below middle C and listen to the speed of the beats.

Under ideal circumstances (the right piano and the right space), it is possible to tune the stretch so that the harmonics actually are the same pitch, as in the first example, so that purely tuned fifths can actually be used, rather than the purely tuned octaves. However, ideal circumstances rarely present themselves. Instead, we try to strike a balance so that although we may not be hitting the harmonics dead-on, we are at least in the ballpark.

This is not as hard to do as it may seem, but like everything else it takes practice. In theory, you will simply try to strike a balance between a pure-sounding fifth and a pure-sounding octave, and try to make each octave above and below the temperament beat purely to the temperament octave.

In practice, it is often hard to hear the difference between a pure double or triple octave and one that is flat or sharp. The trick is to use checks, just as we did in the temperament.

After you have stripped the whole piano and set your temperament, begin the octaves by tuning the first note after the temperament (i.e. the G above middle C.) Tune this note and the rest of its octave by setting each note sharp of perfect to the point where the fifths are as pure as possible, but the octave does not beat noticeably.

When you reach the C above middle C, check it with the double fifth or "Twelfth", which is the bottom F in the temperament octave. Ideally you should be able to make this interval beatless without causing too much activity in the octave and fifth.

Because of the distance between these two notes, you will need both hands to play, so you cannot actually use this interval to tune. However, as you continue up, using the octave and the fifth, keep checking the twelfth for purity.

Once you reach the G two octaves above middle C, you will have to start to make the octaves beat more noticeably in order to make the fifths pure. This isn't a problem; in fact, you can probably increase the purity of the fifth and the twelve without the octaves sounding unacceptable.

The goal is, as you tune farther away from the middle of the keyboard, you keep trying to match the note you are tuning with its match in the temperament octave whether in the treble or in the bass. As you go, make sure you are checking these larger intervals rather than relying on the octave. Use it as a reference, but don't try to make it perfect.

If you encounter a note that sounds good with the temperament octave, but screams with the Perfect Octave, make sure that you haven't made a mistake earlier on.

Everything should progress evenly as you go. If something sticks out, then it is a clue that something earlier is wrong.

Octave Tuning in the High Treble

In the last octave, a note tuned pure to the octave below is more likely to be perceived as flat to the trained ear than if it is actually tuned sharp of perfect.

An easy way to tune the section is to raise it very sharp of the octave, and play its corresponding note in the temperament octave. Give the note a hard blow and check. If it is still sharp, slack-tip tap it down a tiny bit, give it a hard blow, and check it again.

It takes such a microscopic movement in the tension of these short strings to change pitch, that often you can literally pound them onto pitch. This, of course, is provided that you raised the note a reasonable amount.

After a few notes, you should be able to roughly

guess how sharp to raise the note so that two or three hard blows set it in place.

Octave Tuning in the Low Bass

This is the most common problem area for beginning tuners.

It is very easy in the beginning to so misjudge the pitch of the bottom octave strings (especially in small pianos), that you could accidentally raise the pitch many semitones too sharp. This could cause the windings in the string to loosen, or the string to break.

The short, low bass strings can give a mirage of beatlessness, especially if they are double-wound. The reason for this has to do with the effect of scaling on harmonics.

You have probably heard that the bigger the piano, the better the sound. This has nothing to do with volume. A string's pitch is determined by three factors: its speaking length, its thickness, and its tension. To get a short bass string to sound the same pitch as its corresponding note in a large string, these factors have to be altered. To decrease the tension would cause a loss of tone, so therefore, the string is made thicker. The thicker the string, the more stiff it becomes.

Tone is dependent on the string vibrating in

smooth oscillations called sine waves. At certain points of the string, called "nodes", these waves double. When you place your finger on the string to hear the harmonics, you are actually touching a node point. In between the node points the vibrating string creates a

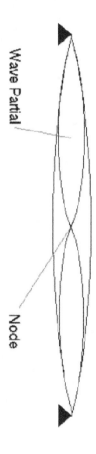

super-oscillation called a wave partial. When a string is stiff, it inhibits the proper formation of the wave partials causing their node points to not line up. This causes each of the super-oscillations to form their own partials.

When a bass string is wildly off-pitch, you can get that illusion of beatlessness because you are hearing a false-partial line up with your reference note. To avoid making a big mistake in the bass, sub-divide each string with your finger to hear the first partial, and go down the scale in semitones. Check each note against the octave or double octave to ensure that it is close to being on pitch. Now when you tune, you know that only a small adjustment is needed to tune each string.

A very common mistake that many tuners make, whether new or experienced, is to hear the quite clear alignment when the string is in tune with the octave above. To make the stretch, you have to lower it below this point.

On most pianos you will actually hear a new beat pattern appear which will slow down to nothing as the twelfth partial begins to coincide with the temperament octave. If it sounds too flat to you at this point, sub-divide the string and listen to the harmonic. It should match the same note played in the temperament.

Sometimes, the acoustics of the piano and the room make this stretch too obvious. In that case, compromise a little towards perfect so that the harmonic aligns with the double octave.

The Unisons

Proper tuning of the unisons is crucial, for practically every customer will be annoyed by poor unisons, and they are often the first thing that slips in a poor tuning.

Problems in unison tuning often occur in the bichords of the bass and the upper trichords in the treble. Loose or poorly made windings, or poor scaling, can cause unisons in wound strings to sound out-of-tune even if they are not - as can false beats in the treble. Therefore, a good tuner must be prepared to deal with these potential problems as part of the tuning procedure.

As was stated earlier, the unisons are tuned starting in the bass, by pulling out the temperament strip one note at a time. This is continued until the top of the middle section has been reached. Then, the octaves in the top treble are checked before completing the tuning of the rest of the unisons.

It is a common mistake for tuners to play softly

as they tune the unisons. This may be because, when tuners are just learning, they soon find out that if they play a note hard while tuning unisons, it can de-tune the source note tuned previously.

It is easy, therefore, to get into the habit of tuning unisons softly. However, if the pins have been properly set during the temperament and octave stage, the danger of slippage is minimized.

A good habit to develop is to tune one side of the unison (always using the aforementioned "soft" blow), and then just before removing the strip loop and tuning the next note, quickly check the now pure unisons against the octave.

Unison Tuning in the Low Bass

The most commonly encountered problem in this area is a bichord that refuses to stop beating. First, check each string individually and listen carefully to see if it beats all by itself. This is relatively common in inexpensive pianos.

The cause of this is usually in the manufacturing process:

When the bass strings are installed, they need to have two or three half-twists in the direction of the winding. This not only keeps the winding tight on the core, but also prevents the string from being unwound during the stringing process.

To explain why this happens, you need to know how bass strings are made.

Traditionally, a string is made by stretching a core wire onto a device remarkably similar to a wood lathe. The core is looped at one end, and the loop is put on a hook attached to a bearing called a "Freewheel".

The other end of the core wire is then clamped into a vise at the other end of the lathe, and stretched to about 200 pounds per square inch.

A small anvil is then placed under the string, and the string is slightly flattened at the points where the winding starts and stops.

The core is then turned at a slow speed by a motor, and the winding is guided under tension onto the core by hand.

When the winding on has been completed, the ends of the winding are molded closed by "Swedging": An anvil with a special groove is placed under the ends, and a hammer is used to pound the ends of the windings together.

When the newly made string is released from the pressure of the lathe, the winding causes the string to coil slightly. The act of putting the string back under pressure in the piano, straightens the string, and that slight coil is transferred into a twisting motion to the core. Therefore, the string has to be twisted at least a little to actually make it straight.

An additional twist is given to the string to ensure that the winding does not loosen, and one more twist increases the volume of the partials by interfering with the way the string vibrates.

Make sure that the string has these two or three half-twists in the direction of the winding. If you are unsure about which direction the twist is to be made, look at the end of the string with a magnifying glass. The end of the winding literally points in the same direction as the twist to be made.

It is the string-maker's job to make sure beforehand that the core has no kinks, nicks or bends, and that the freewheel on the string lathe turns smoothly under pressure.

Modern string-making machines are powered on both ends of the lathe, so, theoretically, if the core is twisted before winding, it is purely the fault of the person installing the core on the lathe. If this is the cause of a false beat in a single wound string, the only solution is to replace it.

If the false beat is very slight, it is sometimes possible to cancel out the false beat by putting a small beat in the unisons in the opposite direction. This involves very carefully "playing" with the tuning of the two strings (i.e. muting the bad string, tuning the good string to the octave, and then tuning the bad string a little sharp or flat of the unison). Sometimes this works, sometimes it doesn't.

It is always best to have a new string made if a string has such a poor sound that it is difficult to tune, and ideally, bi-chords should be remade as a set.

To do this, measure the diameter of the core and the winding, then measure the distance in millimetres from the inside end of the anchor loop, to the start of the winding, and then the length of the winding. A string maker can use these four measurements to make a new string. Many string-makers ask for the note and string number, as well.

Before you rip the string out of the piano, however, make sure that the cause of the false beat isn't because of improper seating on the bridge.

Lightly tap the string into the crotch of the bridge pins with the end of a hammer shank. You can also tap the string very lightly down onto the bridge cap, as well, but make sure that you don't bury the string into the wood.

Unison Tuning in the High Treble

The plain wire strings in the treble often have false beats. This is because it only takes a very small amount of distress in the higher strings to affect their vibrating characteristics. A small bend, nick or twist in the wire can easily cause a false beat.

The most common fault is the string not seating properly on the bridge or the agraffe/nut. The next most common problem is the string receiving a bend as it passes around the bridge pin while flat. Then, when the string is pulled up to pitch, this bend becomes part of the speaking length. To correct this, use the end of a hammer shank to rub the bend out while the string is slightly sharp.

Another problem is the string being twisted during stringing. The only way to check if this is a problem is to loosen the string, pull the coil off the pin, and see if it twists. If it rotates a half a turn or more, then replace the string with a new one. If it stays straight or rotates only slightly, then the string is not twisted. However, it could be brittle or bent, so a replacement is probably a good idea.

One last possibility for false beats in plain wire is poor metal in the string. If the string is noticeably a different color than the rest, or if it is rusty, it should be replaced. If the tine breaks off the becket when removing the string, it is a sure sign that the string is brittle.

Often, time and budget restraints dictate how much tuning-related repair can be done. If it is the case that the above faults exist in the piano but a repair cannot be made, then the tuner is left with no choice but to do the best job he or she can.

Pitch Raising and Lowering

Common sense tells us that the closer a piano is to being on pitch, the more stable the final tuning is going to be. Therefore, if a piano is very flat or sharp, the pitch must be centralized before it is tuned.

How off-pitch must it be before a "pre-tuning" is needed? There is no real hard and fast answer. The better a piano is built and designed, the more stable it will be. Therefore, the point at which it is too far off-pitch is very different for pianos of different qualities.

Using a temperament strip to mute all unisons gives a very good indication when a piano MUST be pitch raised: If the muted unisons are so off-pitch as to be heard when played, then a pitch raise must be done. However, the shorter strings in the high treble mute so well, that you might not notice if it is just that section that is out.

If the bass section is badly out, but the top section is fine, raising the pitch in the bass could affect the tuning in the top end.

If the treble is quite flat or sharp, neglecting to stabilize the pitch first will almost certainly mean that fine-tuning will be a waste of time. Therefore, if there is any doubt, it is safer to pitch raise.

The Pitch Raise

The first step is to ascertain how flat the piano is.

Use your pitch fork to tune either middle C or the A above. Next, play all the C's or A's against the note you tuned, and find the flattest section. Tune the octave above your reference note sharp, so that it beats against the reference note at the same rate as against the flattest note. This note will now be half as sharp as the piano is flat.

NOTE: *There is a limit to how far you can raise the pitch of the piano. An increase of 50 cents adds an incremental amount more in stress than the same amount at a lower pitch. I try to raise the pitch no more than 25 cents sharp of concert-pitch.*

The object of setting the sharp pitch is not to "counteract" the flatness, but to compensate for how much the pitch will drop during the pitch raise.

For example: If you pitch-raised a piano that was 50 cents flat, up to concert pitch, by the time the tuning was done it will drop about 20 cents. If you pull the same piano up 75 cents to 25 cents sharp, by the time you finished, the piano will be close to concert-pitch or sharper by 5 or so cents.

If the same piano was 200 cents flat, pulling up the pitch 300 cents may leave the piano too sharp, or damage the piano in the process. With experience, you soon begin to sense what is too big a raise for the piano.

To be on the safe side, try not to raise the pitch more than 25 cents sharp in one pass.

Better-quality pianos may need much less of a raise above concert-pitch to make them stable. If you are in doubt, raise the pitch just a little above and be prepared to make two passes.

Strip all the unisons, except the top treble sections in an upright. Set a very rough and quick temperament to the concert-pitch note you tuned with you fork. Use this temperament to pull up the wound strings to concert-pitch. Leave the strip in the bass.

NOTE: **Wound strings should never be pulled up sharp as this can cause the winding to separate from the core, resulting in a buzzing string.**

Next, tune a new temperament as quickly as possible to the note you tuned sharp of concert-pitch.

You want it to be reasonably accurate, but you needn't spend a lot of energy on it: The pitch raise will destroy any hard work you put into it. (Plus, in order for a pitch raise to be effective and cost-efficient, it must be done quickly.)

It is important to note that in a pitch raise, time is of the essence. Don't worry too much about setting the pin; just make sure that the pin moves in the block enough to bring it slightly above pitch. When you release tension on the pin, the note should fall down close to the desired pitch.

Next, pull up the middle strings of the middle section using octaves off the temperament. In a grand piano, you can continue into the treble sections, but instead of tuning to an octave, tune to a perfect fifth up until you reach an octave above the middle section.

Tuning to the fifth will make the treble section increasingly sharp.

This is important, because as you raise the pitch of the rest of the piano, the treble will flatten more due to the added stress than will the rest. After you have tuned up to an octave above the middle, you can go back to the bass and pull out the temperament strip, tuning the unisons until you reach the point in the treble where you left off. Finally, tune the remaining treble strings to the octave below.

NOTE: *If the piano is VERY flat, perhaps due to stringing or Tuning Pin Resetting, you may want to consider tuning a rough temperament and then tuning each note an octave at a time in order to spread the stress across the piano.*

In very cheap uprights, the stress of a big pitch raise can, in rare instances, cause the plate to break.

I have seen this happen to other tuners three times during the last forty-odd years. Two of those times, it was a Lesage upright built in the early sixties.

To avoid this possibility, tune the temperament, and then all of the "F's" down in the bass, and then all the "F's" up into the treble, then all the "F#'s", "G's", etc.

In an upright piano, because the top treble is not stripped, you can, while you are learning, use either a rubber mute or a Papp's mute.

It is important, though, that you use the mute so that you are tuning the strings in order, and not using the Papp's mute to tune the centre strings first. This is done only while touching up a drifted octave, not while tuning or pitch raising.

Ideally, however, there is a much faster way to pitch raise in the treble, but it does take practice and concentration: Muteless Tuning.

Muteless Tuning

The three strings in the unison can be individually raised 25 cents or more without mutes. This not only is a great timesaver, but it also can be fun because of the challenge involved.

Basically, the principle behind it is this: Normally when we tune, we listen to the sound of beating between two notes. In muteless tuning, we ignore the beats, and instead, listen to the sound of an individual string moving up in pitch. We can estimate roughly the pitch of the note when we hear it slide up until it stops moving. At that point, because we have brought it above pitch, it is so different from the other notes that it stands out.

First, play the octave below the note that is to be tuned, and remember that pitch. Starting with the left-hand unison in the note to be tuned, pull it up in pitch while playing the note repeatedly. Stop raising the pitch when it reaches the point that it seems a little sharper than the reference note we played first.

Next, raise the middle string of the unison until it sounds pure with the first string. In order to hear this, you have to ignore the sound of the right-hand string, and listen instead to the sound of the string coming up to "meet" the left-hand string.

If you are unsure at first, either pluck the strings to hear their pitch individually, or use your mute. With practice, you will soon be able to hear all three strings at the same time and guess fairly accurately what their pitch is in relation to your reference note, and to each other.

You have three goals to meet during the pitch raise: Speed; a sharp treble; and pulling up the bass only up to pitch. Your eventual goal is to leave the piano on-pitch or slightly above.

Pitch Lowering

The two most commons reasons to lower the pitch of a piano are: Correction of an overshot pitch raise, and correction of the effect of an extreme raise in humidity since the last tuning.

Normally, an overzealous pitch raise results in high pitch just in the top treble. However, if the pitch raise is started too high, it can affect the whole piano (but hopefully not the wound strings).

An increase of pitch due to high humidity is normally not as extreme, and is generalized across the instrument. Sometimes, an increase in humidity can result in an especial sharpness in the tenor strings just above the section break, or the top treble.

Generally speaking, the pitch of each section is lowered just as a normal tuning would be accomplished. Although, if the pitch of the top treble is extremely high, it would be wise to stop at the top and work down so that you don't put undue stress on the highest strings as you reduce the tension of the lower strings.

Feel the pin turn in the block as you lower the pitch slightly below where you want it. Hopefully, when you release the tension of your tuning hammer from the pin, the note should rise up to the desired pitch.

Once again, the goal is speed rather than accuracy, and leaving the piano at a pitch centre where fine-tuning will be stable.

It is impossible to tune a piano perfectly. Even if you have done the best job imaginable, the tuning will drift because of environmental reasons and there is nothing you can do about it.

All that conscientious tuners can do, is to do the

best job they can, in the situation they are given. To obsess about perfection in a situation where perfection is fleeting, is futile.

The Art of Compromise lies in a tuner's ability to take an imperfect instrument and make it the best it can be.

Additional Exercises

In order to tune quickly and accurately, every piano tuner should spend some time practicing the three subjects covered in this section: Keyboard Technique, Ear Training, and Speed/Accuracy Drills. They are all related, and one way or another, practicing one will improve the others.

I also believe that it is a good idea that the tuner who doesn't play the piano should learn at least one song to play after the job is finished. The customer expects it, and it is like the exclamation mark at the end of a sentence!

The whole tuning experience for the technician becomes a journey with a goal.

I promise you that in a relatively short period of time, you will play your one piece with the panache of a pro.

My brother, John, an excellent guitarist and

piano tuner, taught himself to play Beethoven's "Für Elise", and now that he has been playing it everyday for years, plays it better than any pro on record.

I would encourage you to practice these exercises diligently. Having taught music for over forty years, I know that the worst students are often the adults. However, their excuse is always "I couldn't find the time to practice." The tuner has no such excuse. Every day, you play the piano as a trade; every day, you are practicing.

Many of these exercises can be fit into your tuning as part of the job. The customer will probably not notice, and you won't even notice how hard you have actually worked on them. All you will see is how much you have improved and how fast it has happened.

Keyboard Technique

Music is a language, just like English, French or Chinese.

Think for a moment how you learned to speak your mother tongue.

The very first step was hearing the people around you speak.

The second step was learning to understand

some of these sounds you heard and making similar noises.

The third step was making the same noises in the same order and inflection, and understanding what you say, and what you hear, as well.

The fourth step was a long period of increasing how many words you knew to the point where the spoken language is simply a part of who you are.

The fifth step was learning how to read and write. The sixth step was learning how to express your thoughts in written form, so that no matter who read it, they would know something about you and what you were thinking.

You can be just as fluent in music as you are in language. All it takes is patience, and the willingness to make the effort that each step requires.

Music as a Second Language

Here are the previously mentioned stages of fluency broken down into a list, and related directly towards learning music as a second language:

The Listening Stage

An infant needs the first two years of life to pass through this first stage because of their developing brain. For an adult, it is a much shorter period.

Studies done in total immersion language teaching have shown that most people need between four to six weeks of exposure to another language for the sound and syntax of the language to be absorbed by the adult mind.

Luckily, you don't have to go to another country to experience music. Music is more prevalent in western culture than most people even realize. Not only is it a form of entertainment, but it has also become the background to our daily lives. From elevators to movies, we are constantly exposed to the language of music. However, many of us ignore it. We "tune" it out.

As music students, we can make a conscious effort to listen to the music around us, and become aware of the sound and syntax of the musical language.

One way to define music is to say that it is pitch and rhythm organized in time.

The untrained musical ear is attuned to the concept of "Melody" – the tune you sing along to - but music is much more than that.

When you listen to music, you should try to listen for all the other aspects of the whole – other instruments, other voices, the rhythm, and the form.

The form of music is one of the best keys to understanding a piece of music.

Think of the form of music like the structure of a story. Every story is made up of many things, and being literate, we can easily break it down into the smallest parts: Letters make words, words make sentences, and sentences make paragraphs. Every sentence contains a subject and a predicate: i.e. John likes ice cream. John is the subject, and what he likes is the predicate.

Every paragraph contains a complete thought. When we speak, read or write, we rarely think about all these details; however, they still exist, and that is what makes a language.

In every piece of music there are notes. Notes make up sequences, sequences make phrases, and phrases make up melody. The notes have other notes along with them to make chords. They have a rhythm to them just like speech. Finally, all the notes, chords, sequences, and phrases have a structure that organizes them together and makes them logical to the listener.

They are usually organized into sections that can be identified as being unique or repeated – they have a beginning, middle, and an end. Best of all, as far as understanding them goes, they are often accompanied by words, and organized into genre.

The form of a pop song, for instance, can be easily broken down into sections, and the instrumentation and rhythm are recognizable to the untrained ear. Music of other genres, and even cultures, can be broken down and analyzed in the same way, but sometimes, it takes a little more training.

Take the time to really listen to the music around you, and start thinking about what you are hearing in terms of these concepts. Listen to what the drummer is doing, or the bass player, or any other part of the song other than the melody.

Believe it or not, the only difference between a musician and a non-musician (in the pop music world, at least), is that musicians listen, and try to understand what is happening in the song they are listening to.

Even the most amateurish songwriter knows that every song has a form, and instrumentation, and a rhythm. They have taken the time to go through the steps and gain at least some form of fluency in the language of music.

The Noisemaking Stage

Besides being a cute sound to the parents, or a cry of hunger, babies make noise because they are experimenting with the sounds they can make themselves. They play with these noises until they begin to form sounds recognizable as language.

The fact of the matter is that this is actually fun for infants. They love to hear the sound of their own voice. (Some never grow out of this stage.)

This stage in learning music can be fun, as well. No baby is ever embarrassed about going through the ga-ga-go-goo stage. Neither should we. Luckily, we can be alone while we do it.

When an infant vocalizes, two distinct things are happening: They are exercising their vocal chords, preparing them to make the right sounds, and they are learning how to control these sounds.

This second stage for a beginning pianist is fairly simple, but important. What you have to do is prepare your fingers to work in the right way to make music.

This is how it's done:

Sit up straight at the keyboard at a height so that when your fingers are on the keys, your forearms are parallel to the floor.

Put each of your fingers on a key so that each hand has five fingers on five keys comfortably.

The keys are played by the fingertips only. Your knuckles should be curled, and the backs of your hands in line with your forearms. (Piano teachers have been known to tape rulers across the forearm, wrist, and the back of the hand to ensure that this rule is not broken.)

When you play the keys, use the weight of your arms. **Do not lift your fingers off the keys!** Raise your knuckles, **(don't raise your wrist!)**, straighten your fingers slightly, and let the weight of your arms play the keys. Your fingers and wrists have to be relaxed, and act like little shock-absorbers as the weight of your arms bring them downwards.

Practice this motion until it is second nature. Relaxed and tensionless, your hands merely position your fingers – the arms do all the work.

When the mechanics of this exercise are firmly ingrained into your hands and mind, practice doing the same thing on a different set of keys, then changing sets each time. Think about your posture, your hand and arm position, and most of all, think about keeping tension out of your hands and wrists.

The next exercise is to do exactly the same process, but this time lifting your hands six inches into the air, and bringing the fingers down on the keys you want, never letting any tense up, and using your fingers as shock-absorbers.

Spend fifteen minutes a day for two weeks doing this. Follow the rules, and above all – have fun making some noise! By the time you have finished this stage, your fingers will be one with the keys.

All that is needed to make music now, is "facility" - which musicians call "Technique".

The Imitation Stage

It is a very unfortunate fact that most piano teachers skip this stage. I believe that it is one of the main reasons why some students quit, and many others never learn to play by ear.

There are two steps to this stage: The first is acquiring technique, and the second is experimentation.

Although many students are scared off by the practice of technique, it is actually one of the best parts about music. Practicing technique can be a zen-like experience where your body goes into autopilot and your mind drifts off into someplace else entirely.

In order for this to happen, though, a commitment of time is needed. Like meditation, it will only be enjoyable and relaxing if you commit the time to it and forget everything else.

It doesn't have to be a big commitment of time. In fact, it could be five minutes, three times a day – but it has to be every day, preferably more than once a day, and probably for at least a month or two.

In the previous stage, you got used to having fingers on the keys, playing properly. Now, it's time to make the fingers work individually.

Each of the following points is one step. Be comfortable with each step before moving on.

Take the same sets of keys used earlier, and play them one at a time. It can be in any order, or no order at all; hands separately, or together. In the beginning, the only thing you have to think about is making sure that you don't tense up. If your hands are tense, stop playing and shake the tension lightly out.

Don't play until it hurts! Stop before it hurts, and get to know your limits. Better to spend five minutes or less several times a day, than one big block of time. Babies rarely goo for longer then a few minutes. After a few times, you'll notice that you can do this longer each time.

Try making some kind of order to the notes you are playing. It can be the pattern of notes, or the rhythm. The important thing is that you start to exercise some kind of control over your fingers in a logical and repeatable fashion.

Change your position on the keyboard. Use other notes. Incorporate small intervals and black notes.

The important thing about these initial stages is that they must be repeated over and over, stopping only when you become aware that you are tensing up, or about to get sore. Unlike weightlifting, the rule is "No Pain, Great Gain!"

Invent sequences of notes to practice that may sound familiar in some way. For instance: Five-note scales up and down, or "Doe, a deer a female deer. Ray, a drop of golden sun".

When I was a teenager, I taught myself how to play the five-string banjo by playing the fingerpicking patterns over and over while my Dad and I watched T.V.

It was a measure of my Dad's character that he never asked me to stop. All he would say is, "You're having trouble there. Slow down, son".

Therein lies the key to practicing anything, whether a sequence of notes or an entire piece: Play it slowly until you have mastered it at that speed, then speed up.

If you make a mistake, slow down so that you are a little faster than the speed you can do it at. If you have a metronome, the rule is: Two clicks ahead, and one click back.

Two steps forward and one step back will always get you where you are going if you have patience.

Practice sequences where your thumb crosses under your finger to play a note.

The technical secret to playing anything on the piano is fingering. The secret to fingering is that your thumb crosses under your fingers, or your fingers over your thumb. Fingers never cross over fingers.

Normally, the practice of technique is associated with playing scales. However, I think of scales as being part of the process of acquainting one's ear and technique with a specific key signature.

If you want to learn some scales, get a scale book and practice them with the right fingering. Don't try to fake it. There is really no point and it is probably counterproductive.

The important things in this stage are:
1. Regular practice.
2. Repetitive motions.
3. Proper posture and hand positions.
4. No Pain, Great Gain.
5. Experimenting with patterns and rhythms.

Now, for the Experimental part of the Imitation Stage: Your fingers are now accustomed to playing the keys, and your brain has some ability to control them.

Use this hard-won facility to try to play some of the music you know and hear. Think of a song and hum the melody. Find the notes you are humming on the keyboard, and practice getting them in the right order, then the right rhythm, then the right tempo. In doing this, you are training your fingers, your ear, and your mind.

Always remember: Proper posture and hand position, "No Pain, Great Gain", and "Two clicks forward, one click back".

The Speaking Stage

This stage is a long period of time invested into being able to play more pieces by ear. Not just the melody, but also the bass line of songs, the vocal harmonies, the chords used, and even the rhythm of the drums – either on the keyboard or tapped with your hand on your knees.

It is possible to go through this stage on your own, but it is faster and easier if you have some guidance. It is almost always possible to find a music teacher who will teach you in exchange for your tuning services. The key is to find someone you like, who can relate to you, and is willing to teach you to play by ear.

The ideal piano teacher has three qualities: They must be a musician, fluent in music, and not just a pianist. They must teach you music, not just piano, and they must be enthusiastic about what they do. If they love music, and love teaching, you'll probably love being taught music by them.

The Reading and Writing Stage

This also requires some guidance, although it is easier to teach yourself how to be musically literate than it would seem. In fact, this process is easier than the speaking stage, providing you actually went through that stage first.

Learning how to read and write music before learning how to play is like trying to teach someone to read and write a language before they can speak it. It makes no sense, and becomes an academic exercise rather than a practical skill.

In order for you to finish this chapter, you will need to know a little about reading music. These are very rudimentary lessons, enough for you to explore further exercises in tuning, but just scratching the surface.

In language terms, reading music goes from "See Dick, see Jane" to Shakespeare, to mathematical theorems. There is always more to learn, more complexities to grasp.

For the purposes of this book, we'll stick to "Dick and Jane". Music is written on paper in a way that it shows both pitch and rhythm. Remember, music is pitch and rhythm organized in time. It is a type of graph in a way. The X-axis shows the pitch, the Y-axis, the time.

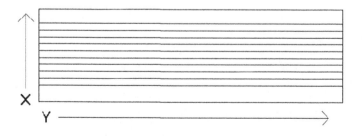

The higher up the X-axis a note is placed, the higher the pitch; the farther along the Y-axis, the further along in time. The number of lines in this graph represents specific keys on the keyboard. In order to make it easier to read, the graph is split apart at middle C.

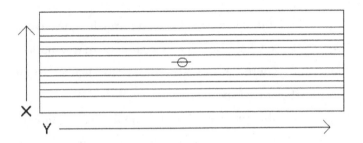

Middle C itself is between these two split-apart sections. Whenever a C is to be written, you not only write the note in the middle, but you put in the missing line.

In order to further help you identify which note goes on what line, you add signs at the beginning of the graph, which are called "Clefs".

The graph that represents the keyboard above middle C gets a "Treble Clef" or "G Clef". It is called this because it is an old fashioned way of writing a capital G, and it literally curls around the line that represents the G above middle C. Any note written on this line, therefore, is a G.

The graph that represents the notes on the keyboard below middle C has a sign at the beginning called a "Bass Clef" or an "F Clef". Once again, this sign is an old-fashioned stylized capital F. Instead of the two arms sticking out like our F, it has two dots. These dots are on either side of the line that represents the F below middle C. Therefore, any note put on this line will be that F.

Put together, the two graphs or "Staffs" are called a "Stave", which looks like this:

Now you know where on the stave is the F below middle C, middle C itself, and the G above, but what are the other lines? Well, the lines each represent a note, but so do the spaces between them. Here's an easy way to remember which lines represent which note:

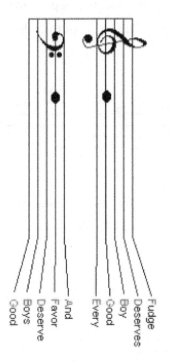

As you can see, the lines represent from the bottom up: G, B, D, F, and A below middle C, and E, G, B, D, and F above middle C. In between those lines are the rest of the notes.

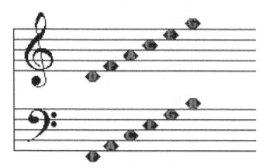

Now you know the rudiments of how pitch is written down. Using what you have just learned, we can take the Temperament Pattern #1 "Chasing the Tail" and write it down as notes.

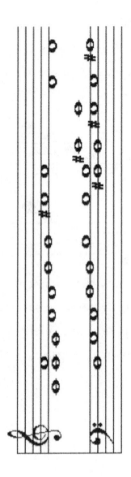

The Whole Note. The whole note gets four beats. It's called a whole note because in the time signature of 4/4 or "Common Time", four beats is the entire, or whole, measure.

The Half Note. The half note gets two beats, or "half" of a measure.

The Quarter Note. The quarter note gets one beat, or a quarter of a four beat measure.

The Eighth Note. The eighth note gets a half of a beat, or one-eighth of a measure.

Any of these notes can be increased in length by half of its value by adding a little dot after the note. Therefore, a "dotted" half note gets three beats instead of two.

If, at the beginning of a stave, we see the time signature 4/4 or a "C" (for common time), we note that there is four beats to a measure, and a quarter note (the bottom four of the time signature) gets one beat.

The following example shows four measures in common time. Each measure has the right amount of notes adding up to four beats; however, apart from the first two bars, a little simple math is needed to prove that statement true.

The easy way to figure out the rhythm of the notes is to count the beats. To count the eighth notes, which get half a beat, we say "and".

I can write out the same rhythm with words. Just say the following at an even beat:

One and two and three and four and, **one** and **two** and **three** and **four** and, **one** and two and **three** and **four and**, **one** and two **and three and** four **and**.

Just say the bold words louder than the rest, and you hear the rhythm notated below.

Notice that I wrote out "and", even when there are no eighth notes in the measure. Saying: "One and Two and" will help you keep the beats and notes in the right places.

So, now you know how pitch and rhythm are notated. Play the following example: Remember, anything is easy if you break it down into smaller bits.

Figure out the pitch of the notes, then which fingers play them, then the rhythm, then put it all together starting slowly, and getting faster.

Hopefully, you will recognize this tune. (I may have to write a different example for the international versions of this book!)

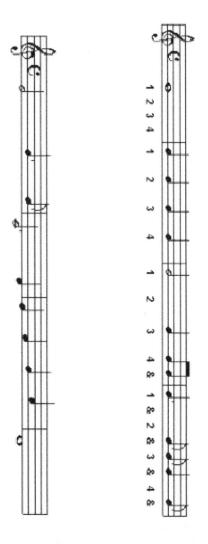

Remember the way your hands were positioned on the keys in the early noisemaking stage of learning. Each finger has a key, but if you HAVE to cross over, fingers over the thumb, or thumb under the fingers!

When there is a full stave (two staffs), the upper staff (the treble) is played by the right hand. The bottom staff (the bass) is played by the left hand. Here is the end of the above piece, but played with the left hand:

In most simple pieces of music, the left hand plays a bass line, and sometimes some harmony. Here are the first four bars again, but this time with a full stave, melody, bass (and harmony):

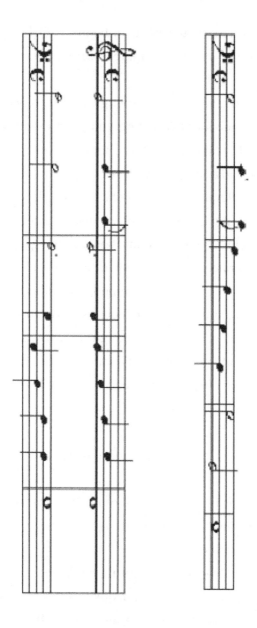

There are hundreds of books available for easy piano. If you would like more examples, pick up a few to practice with.

An alternative to buying easy piano books is to use a hymnbook. Everything you need to know about keyboard playing, theory, harmony and form is contained in a single hymnbook.

I literally taught myself how to play the piano and read music by starting at the beginning of the United Church's Red Hymn book, playing each vocal part separately, then together, and pushing myself through to the end. By the time I had finished, I could sight read anything, understood harmony and notation, and played piano well enough to enter the music program at the University of Calgary. The entire process from beginning to end only took me less than two years!

The Expression Stage

This is the final stage of fluency. Once you have a good grasp of the language of music, you can compose your own.

I know that many of us think up catchy tunes, but if you can't write them down, they are just folk-songs to be passed along (or kept to oneself.)

For a poet to be a poet, an author to be an author, or a composer to be a composer, they have to be able to write their compositions down. This stage, like its corollary in language, is best learned from a qualified teacher.

Keyboard Training Exercises

In order to smoothly test consecutive intervals, practice the following exercises until you can perform them quickly and effortlessly. Make sure you follow the directions exactly and use the proper fingering!

Chromatic Scales

Playing each semitone in a row, up or down, is referred to as a chromatic scale. The proper hand position is essential in order to play the scale quickly. In order to see this position and "get the feel" of it, Take your right hand and place your fingers on a table in the proper hand position for playing. Put the thumb, first, and second finger side by side and slightly lift your ring finger and little finger off the table. Now move your elbow slightly off to the right.

Take that same hand position and move it onto the keyboard so that your thumb finger is on middle C, and your middle finger is on C#.

Now, take your left hand and place your fingers on a table just like you did for your right hand. Put the thumb, first, and index finger side by side and slightly lift your ring finger and little finger off the table. Now move your elbow slightly off to the left.

Take that same hand position and move it onto the keyboard so that your middle finger is on middle C, and your thumb is on B.

From C going up, this is the fingering for the chromatic scale: Thumb, middle, thumb, middle, thumb, index, middle, thumb, middle, thumb, middle, thumb, etc. The only keys the index finger plays are the F's and the C's.

From top C going down, this is the right-hand fingering for the chromatic scale: Middle, thumb, middle, thumb, middle, thumb, middle, index, thumb, middle, thumb, middle, index, etc.

NOTE: As a general rule, all scales are played so that the thumb only plays white keys, and never the black keys.

To play a chromatic scale going down with your left hand, start on middle C with your thumb, then index, middle, thumb, middle, thumb, middle, thumb, index, middle, thumb, middle, etc.

It's the same pattern as going up, but in reverse. Notice that the two hands have the same fingering.

Start slowly, and only speed up as you gain proficiency. "Two clicks up, one click back."

Chromatic Scales in Octaves

Now practice the chromatic scales with both hands together. Notice that when the right hand's thumb is playing a key, the left hand's thumb is doing the same.

Be very diligent with practicing this scale. Start very slowly, preferably using a metronome. When you have a speed mastered, then speed up two clicks. Go back one click if you make a mistake. Practice until you can play this scale with both hands as fast as you can with one.

Various Parallel Intervals

Using a metronome, practice doing scales of the various tuning intervals: Twelfths, tenths, sixths, fifths, fourths and thirds. Make sure you use the proper fingering in each hand as learned in the previous exercises.

This is a little trickier because the thumbs and fingers are no longer doing the same thing at the same time. Use the metronome, and increase your speed slowly.

Ear Training

Learning to tune in itself is ear training. However, just hearing beats is not all that the professional tuner needs to be able to do.

In this chapter, you will find exercises designed to help you refine your listening skills, and help you to understand what it is you are actually hearing.

The following is a list of all the individual aspects of a tuning that the tuner must recognize and understand. For each item, I have included an exercise. Practice these while you are learning, and again after you have been tuning for a short period of time.

Not only will they help students learning to tune, but they will also help refine the skills of the professional tuner, and serving as a guide to how far you have progressed.

Perfect Pitch

I have been asked many times over the years if I must have "Perfect Pitch" to tune a piano. Of course, the answer is no. However, the very fact that they asked the question in the first place proves that they don't understand the concept of "Perfect Pitch".

The perfect pitch that most people are familiar with is the ability to identify the pitch of a note without a reference. Often this means not only if a note is a C or an F#, but also if it is "In Tune". In many ways, this ability is nothing more than a kind of parlour trick. It is impressive to those who can't do it, and especially impressive to those who wish they could.

For most people, the ability to identify notes out of thin air is a hard-won learned skill. But, for a lucky few, it is a talent that seemed to develop overnight.

Once again, it is like language. In a sample population, there are always people who have a natural ability with language, either as a writer, or as a public speaker. Sometimes these abilities seem effortless, but the truth is that even the talented have to work at honing their skills.

The secret is that the real talent lies in having such a great interest in the subject, that even the studying and hard work involved in mastering the skill is enjoyable - even exciting.

There are different types of "Perfect Pitch". The most common among musicians is called "Acquired Relative Pitch". This is the skill, learned through experience and practice, of being able to identify any pitch by using one starting pitch, and finding any other by using a reference.

For instance, a singer should be able to look at a piece of written music and sing what is written by just knowing the key of the music and being given a starting pitch. When you think of it, this is not such a difficult task. Most of us can sing a song we know without music. A musician is simply reading what is written and singing just as if it were a story read out loud.

Having Acquired Relative Pitch also means, that if you gave a singer a C, and told them to sing an F#, they could do it. This is simply a learned skill. All you need is the ability to sing in key – if you play a note on the piano, you can sing the same note.

The next most common kind of perfect pitch is called "Perfect Acquired Relative Pitch". This is merely one more refinement in musical skill. It is the ability to discern the pitch of any given note, without a reference.

For instance, being able to tell what pitch a note is without finding it on an instrument. Many instrumentalists develop this skill through repetition. Violinists can often sing an "A" if asked, because every day they tune their instruments using an "A". Trumpet players can sing a Bb, French Horn players, an F. They "learn" the sound of a pitch merely through endless repetition.

Professional guitarists can often sing an "E" on cue, and they also have the learned ability to be able to tell what specific chord another guitarist is using because they recognize the specific combination of notes in that chord.

Jazz players call this "Voicing". There are many ways to play each chord, and all those different ways are different voicings of that chord. This isn't an innate talent – it is the product of years of practicing.

Acquired Perfect Pitch is not as common as the previous instances. However, it is still quite common among the best musicians. Some musicians' ears are so well trained, that they can tell a difference in pitch, without a reference, in terms of cycles per second. They can literally hear the tempering in notes – the difference in pitch of a tempered and non-tempered note – even when both notes are in tune in their own context.

I knew a musician who, when given a random recording of a concert piece, could not only tell you the name and composer of the piece, but he could also tell you if the piano, or the recording, was sharp or flat of concert-pitch; what kind of piano it was; who was playing it; and when it was recorded. This is not a gift. It is the natural by-product of intensive study, endless enthusiasm, and the lack of a normal social life.

Some people with acquired perfect pitch say that they "see" pitch in terms of colour. They have learned to associate the key of a piece of music with a certain hue. F is dark blue, G is green, etc.

True Innate Perfect Pitch is immeasurably rare, and in many ways it is a curse rather than a gift. Having true perfect pitch means that hearing a note, or a combination of notes, that is not perfectly in tune with one another mathematically, is actually painful.

A piano tuner with a keenly trained ear may be annoyed by the sound of an un-tuned piano, but that is only because he can fix the problem. With true perfect pitch, even a well-tuned piano is annoying because it is tempered. These people never become musicians. In fact, they avoid listening to music at all. They have the most in common with people of a slightly less rare disability, Monotonalism.

True monotones lack the ability to either process pitch out of a certain narrow range, or to physically reproduce a normal range of speaking pitches.

Most monotones literally speak monotonally or can't speak at all. Some monotones are classified as deaf, because they can only hear in such a small tonal range.

The classic cop-out of "Oh, I can't sing! I'm tone-deaf" is the ultimate misuse of terminology. If that statement were true, they wouldn't even have to say it. They couldn't hear the question, couldn't speak the answer, or simply would not have been asked. A speaking tone-deaf person is instantly recognizable. All of the normal inflections in speech are absent or severely limited.

When someone says that they are "Tone-Deaf", it usually means that they have never actually listened to the sound of their own voice when they sing. In most cases, an off-key singer can be taught to sing on-key by teaching them how to listen - not only to what they are singing, but how it relates to what they are singing to.

When people ask me if I have perfect pitch, I tell them (with a smile) that I have Qualified Imperfect Acquired Relative Pitch, or "Quiarp". Given enough time and enough hints, I can usually make a close guess as to the pitch of a note – as long as I don't have to be right all the time.

On an average day, the lowest note I can sing comfortably is a D two octaves below middle C, and the highest I can sing is a D an octave above. To identify a note, I'll sing my highest or lowest note and then estimate the interval between my note and the given note.

Sometimes this works, and sometimes it doesn't. What's important is that I can tell if a piano is in tune or not.

Pitch

Exercise #1

Find out for yourself what your vocal range is and practice the somewhat less-than-astounding parlour trick of "Quiarp". Sing your lowest note and your highest note, and find out which notes they are on the piano. Check it out every time you pass a piano keyboard over a few days to make sure that you know what your range actually is. Once you're sure, then do the opposite; sing the two notes and then play the keys. If you do this often enough, you will eventually be able to match those two notes very closely, almost every time.

Exercise #2

I call this the "Bathroom Break Test". The next time you are tuning and have to stop in the middle to visit the washroom, sing softly to yourself the last note you tuned. While you are away from the piano, hum this note every once and a while to yourself. When you return, test to see if you are still humming the same pitch. If you're not, start by almost constantly humming that one note. If you are on pitch, increase the amount of the challenge, i.e. Only hum when you leave and when you return, or hum the next note to be tuned after playing the note before, etc.

Exercise #3

Carry one of your tuning forks with you wherever you go. If you normally use an "A: 440" fork, then carry the "C: 523.3", etc.

Listen to the pitch of the fork as often as you can. Hum or whistle the pitch as you listen. After doing this for a few days, hum or whistle before you play the fork, and see how close you can guess the pitch. Some musicians have told me that this was how they acquired "Perfect Pitch".

The Individual Pitch of One String

Exercise #1

Every once and a while, when you are tuning unisons, pluck the three strings individually and try to identify which string is sharp or flat without playing a reference note. Then, tune the first unison to the reference, pluck the others and try to identify in what way they relate to the now-tuned unison.

Are the others sharp or flat, and by how much?

Tune the remaining unisons by plucking only – muting the other strings each time you pluck. By plucking the strings in this manner, your ability to hear the beats is removed, so you are forced to tune by listening only to their relative pitch. (Make sure to test the setting of the pin before moving on.)

Exercise #2

When doing a big pitch raise in a piano, have a C.D. of music playing in the background – preferably piano music. Play the piece on repeat, find the most dominant note repeated in the piece on another tuned piano or keyboard, and then tune all the keys on the piano that match the note in the piece.

When all the "C's" are tuned, skip to the next track and find a different note. This exercise is a preliminary to an advanced exercise described later in this chapter.

The Sound of Two Strings
Interacting with One Another

Exercise # 1

When tuning a piano that is basically on pitch but with poor unisons, lay in a good temperament, and then strip the remainder of the piano so the strip only mutes every other unison. (i.e. The left string on one note, and the right string of the note above.)

Play your reference note, and tune the octave without muting the other unison. Listen to how the string moves initially.

Do the beats in the unisons get faster or slower? What do the beats between the octave and the two unisons do?

Try to estimate how much and in which way to tune the string in order to get it closer to the octave. Tune the other unison to see if your estimation was correct.

After this has been done a number of times, you should start to hear how the relationship between the two out-of-tune unisons relates to the tuned reference note.

Exercise #2

Prepare the piano as in Exercise #1. Play your reference note, and then tune the unisons by remembering the pitch of the reference. Play the reference as much as you need, but do not play it at the same time as the note you are tuning.

This is a good exercise to prepare you for Muteless Tuning.

The Sound of Three Strings
Interacting with Each Other

Exercises #1 & #2

Repeat the two exercises above without the temperament strip. Use a piano that is severely flat when starting to do these exercises.

Exercise #3

When setting the temperament, tune an octave above the last tuned note, and play both notes while tuning the next interval.

This will work if you have a feel for how narrow or wide you are making the note without having to hear the beats exactly.

The Sound of a Semitone

Exercise #1

I am told that this exercise is commonly given as a test to new or visiting tuners to the Steinway Factory.

Strip the temperament, and tune your starting note and the octave above to your fork. Next, tune each semitone between the two reference notes a semitone at a time. C, C#, D, D#, etc. - without any checks.

When you reach the reference note at the top, see how close or far away your last tuned note is to the reference in comparison to the other semitones.

Most tuners have a tendency to make a semitone too large, making the last note obviously sharp of the top reference.

Start at the beginning again and make each semitone closer together until you manage to end up with a fairly close approximation of semitones from the top to the bottom.

Finally, tune the temperament as you normally would, and pay attention to how far off your last semitone-by-semitone attempt was.

The Sound of the Intervals

As piano tuners, we normally listen for the beats between strings. It is important, however, that we learn the sound of the intervals, and can recognize which intervals are which just by their sound. When pitch raising in fifths, for instance, if we can't recognize a fifth, it makes it almost impossible to bring a severely flat string up into a fifth.

Exercise #1

On a tuned piano, play each of the intervals and try to recognize their sound no matter where on the keyboard.

At first, try very hard to make sure that you have the right interval before you play it.

For instance, if you are going to play a fifth with

the right hand, place your thumb on a note without playing it. Count eight keys up from that note (including the note under your thumb), put your little finger on the eighth note, and then play the interval. Major Third = 5 notes, Perfect Fourth = 6 notes, Major Sixth = 10.

Exercise #2

On a tuned piano, have someone else play the intervals, and without looking, try to figure out what interval it is. It is preferable to do this with someone who knows the intervals themselves.

Exercise #3

Challenge yourself to try to sing the intervals before hearing it. For instance, play a "C", and then try to sing the P5 "G" above, then play the G and see if you're right.

The Sound of Compound Intervals

A compound interval is an interval with more than an octave difference. For instance, a Major third plus an octave is called a "Tenth".

This interval is especially handy when tuning in the lower register. Just as Major thirds slow down as they get lower, the tenths do the same thing.

As large intervals are easier to hear in the bass, the tenth is often used to check the tuning of the octaves in the bass.

The most commonly used compound intervals are the Tenth, the Twelfth (Fifth + Octave), the Fifteenth (Double Octave), and the Nineteenth (Fifth + two Octaves).

Do the three previous exercises with compound intervals. (For Exercise #3, use a lower starting note so you don't hurt yourself!)

The Sound of an Octave

Although this one may seem like a no-brainer, there are two interesting exercises that you can perform if you are comfortable with singing.

Exercise #1

Play a note, sing that note, then stop and sing the octave above. Not only is this good training for singing, but it helps exercise your brain's ability to "visualize" a note.

Exercise #2

Play a note, and then sing the octave above while still holding the note. Purposefully, but slowly, slide the note you are singing slightly sharp, then slightly flat, then on-pitch. Do this with as many different notes as you are comfortable singing.

The Sound of an Octave Stretch

When you are tuning, try this little exercise to check the difference between Perfect and Stretched Octaves:

Exercise #1

After setting the temperament with your "A" fork, tune, in Perfect octaves, all the other A's. When you get to the point that you are tuning those notes during your normal octave tuning, check and see if they are flat according to your temperament.

Exercise #2

If you get the opportunity, tune two similar pianos in similar rooms so that one has a blended nonstretch tuning, and the other has a normal stretch tuning. Have someone play the pianos, stand back, and listen to the difference in the sound. (Better yet, have someone else do the tunings while you fix yourself a drink.)

Speed Drills

Exercise #1

Carry a stopwatch with you when you tune. Check how long it takes you to tune each step: How long for the temperament, the octaves, the unisons, etc. Calculate your average time over ten pianos, and then each subsequent time, challenge yourself to be a little faster.

Exercise #2

Buy a small hourglass-type egg timer and use Cyanoacrylatic (Krazy) Glue to securely fasten the stand on each end. Turn the timer every time you move to a new string.

If you consistently beat the timer every time, carefully drill a tiny hole through one of the bases and let out a little sand. Close the hole with tape, and use the timer again to time how long it takes for you (on average) to tune each string.

Keep letting out a little sand until you reach the point that you have to force yourself to speed up in order to keep up with the timer. If you reach the point where you consistently beat the timer once more, let out some more sand.

NOTE: Most tuners are capable of more speed than they realize. They re-tune notes that are already in tune, they use too many checks, and generally waste time. Trying to "Beat the Clock" will help you see how efficient your skills really are.

Exercise #3

Before you start a tuning, make an educated guess as to how long the tuning will take, based on the quality of the piano and the state of the tuning. After you have finished, check and see how accurate your guess was. Do this enough times so that your guesses become more accurate.

Most tuners underestimate (sometimes wildly) how long their tunings take. Knowing your speed not only helps you organize your day better, but helps you see if your efficiency is improving.

Everything You Ever Wanted To Know
About Pianos But Were Afraid To Ask

EEK! - Piano "Horror" Stories

Notice the quotes? I use the word "horror" with my tongue firmly planted in my cheek. There have definitely been a few pianos I have seen over the past three decades which have been scary, or in scary condition, but for the most part, hindsight has made many a horror story into a comedy.

Some stories, however, are horrific. Over the years I have seen pianos "fixed" with duct tape, "lubricated" with WD-40, moved in pick-up trucks, and worst of all, "rebuilt inside" by being sprayed with gold paint. I'm not kidding. I have seen, and continue to see, ridiculous repairs and farcical fixes such as these.

There is a right way to do everything. Most of the ways, logical and simple. A few of them, expensive and challenging. A good example of this involves an old piano that a Winnipeg businessman had found in a granary near the small town of Boissevain, Manitoba. It was a full upright, built in the States, with a bentwood flamed Honduras mahogany case.

To build such a piano today would cost tens of thousands of dollars, but this man had paid only the cartage to my shop. Anyone seeing this piano in the condition it which arrived would have stepped back in horror, but I saw the potential buried underneath. We took two five-gallon pails full of mouse carcasses, droppings and filth out of that piano, wearing rubber gloves and face masks.   We stripped it down to nothing, until it was reduced to thousands of little bits filling shelves and work benches. Every piece was deodorized, sanitized, cleaned, and repaired, and the case was stripped down, sanded, and treated to twelve coats of hand-rubbed lacquer.

The cost for this project greatly exceeded the cost of a new piano. (Much less, however, than it would have cost to have it re-created.) The most interesting thing to note is that another rebuilder quoted a figure of almost half of what I quoted. To rebuild this piano at that price, corners would have been cut – probably the cleaning. Piano à la mousse, anyone?

I'm often finding interesting things inside of pianos – coins, cards, and toys are common. One piano I opened up contained a small bag of marijuana. I showed it to the owner, and was inwardly amused at the range of emotions that flitted across his face.

I saw surprise, then guilt, then fear, then finally the glint of creativity as he quickly made up the excuse that it was his son's. Around the piano were pictures of his family – not a male child in any of them.

A far more common thing that I find in pianos are the calling cards from the tuners who came before me. When I used to work on older pianos in Winnipeg, I would often see the little round blue-and-white sticker that was my grandfather's, or the gold-and-white rectangular sticker that was my father's. Whenever I saw those, I'd think about where they were, and who they were, when they were there before me. Once, when tuning in Calgary, I saw my father's name in a piano, along with a date: May 11th 1959. That was his 53rd birthday, and the day before I was born.

When I was little, my father routinely did the concert tunings for the Calgary Philharmonic on the stage of the Southern Alberta Jubilee Auditorium. Of course, I often went along. We would enter through the stage door, where the guard would greet us by name, and then, while Dad tuned, I would explore. I knew every nook and cranny of that building like the back of my hand. The stage crew who worked there would often let me sit by them in the lighting booth, the sound booth, or in the stage manager's office.

Sometimes, if I was really lucky, there would be

no one there except my dad and I, and the guard at the door. There were many secret places in that building, and I would pretend I was a spy, infiltrating the "enemy's" secret laboratory. One time, I remember, I sneaked onto the lighting catwalk high above the stage, my father a small speck far below. I loved the adrenalin rush of heights and dangerous places, and revelled in the fantasy that I was one step away from a marvelously romantic obituary.

Dad would have no idea where I wandered, but I knew when it was time to return. He would play a series of scales to check his work when he had finished tuning, and then launch into "The Man I Love". That would be my cue to come back to his side. I remember once sitting in the farthest seat in the top balcony of that huge auditorium as he tuned. I must have been more than a football field's length away, and yet, when I called to him after he had finished his "finale", he heard me and answered softly, "Time to go." I heard him as clear as a bell.

Once I had learned to play the piano, he would ask me to play for him. I would sit at the big black Steinway in that auditorium and imagine the empty seats filled first with an expectant audience, and then with the roar of a standing ovation as I finished. In actuality, my dad would place his hand gently on my shoulder and smile.

That Steinway grand - #354046, built in 1956 - had been in my father's care since it first arrived. Glenn Gould was one of the first pianists to perform on it, and in preparation for that concert, Dad pulled out all the stops to make it perfect for the famous wunderkind.

Just before the concert, after Mr. Gould had practised, my father gave it another quick check. In front of the piano was a ratty, obviously homemade monstrosity of a stool. Without checking, and without thinking, my dad replaced it with the real bench, and threw the chair into the garbage bin outside.

Of course, this was Glenn's famous chair, handmade to his specifications by his father. He threw a major fit, refusing to go on stage until it was found. Finally my dad was asked, and he retrieved it, plunking it down in front of "his" beautiful new Steinway, disgusted. From that day onward, my mother referred to Canada's most celebrated piano virtuoso as "The Kook".

My mother, although an intelligent and respected business woman, harboured a secret "spiritual" side. She believed in ghosts, for example, and, I guess, as her son, I must have inherited that recessive gene. I have had many spooky experiences with pianos - some easily explainable in the light of day, others...

A lady called me one morning, saying that her piano, which I had tuned a few months earlier in the dead of winter, was now inexplicably and horribly out of tune. When I arrived at her door, she had the look of someone who was definitely sleep-deprived. I asked her if she was all right, and she replied that she had spent a sleepless night.

She had had a nightmare, and when she awoke from it, heard the sound of a gunshot coming from the living room directly below her. Then, upon daybreak, she had crept downstairs to find nothing amiss – except that her piano sounded terrible.

A quick check of the piano revealed that the cast-iron plate inside, which holds most of the tremendous stress of all the strings, had snapped in half. The "gunshot" was the sound of the plate snapping.

The piano was a Lesage spinet, a brand known for faulty plates. A recent spate of rainy weather had caused the soundboard to swell, increasing the strain on the piano to its breaking point. It just happened to coincide with her nightmare. Mystery solved.

Not quite as easy to explain is "The Case of the Singing Piano". Many years ago, when I was relatively new to the business, I tuned a piano for an elderly widow who lived in a large house in an "old-money" district. The house, built very much in the "Olde English" style, had faded greatly through neglect, though it was still easy to see that it had once been glorious.

The piano had been cleared off in advance of my call, music books and framed old photographs stacked on the dining room table. As I tuned her old piano, she sat in a chair beside me. When I finished, I asked her if she would like to try it. She replied that she didn't play - the piano was her late husband's - and she had tuned it because he had told her to tune it. So, she asked me to play it for her.

For some reason, I chose to play "Abide With Me". It was not a tune that I usually would play, but it seemed to just be at my fingertips. When I finished, she quietly went to the table, brought back a yellowed piece of music, and placed it on the music rack. It was "Abide With Me", in the key that I had played it.

It was her husband's favourite hymn, and she had heard the piano play the sacred song as she fell asleep the night before, a wholly different kind of tuning reminder.

I have seen many "Piano Miracles" in my day - instances where, through rebuilding, I have brought them back from the dead. However, I have also seen it happen without any intervention at all. During July of 2012, I was honoured to be the sole technician entrusted with the care of the street pianos during the "Play Me, I'm Yours" event, leading up to the 2015 Pan Am Games.

There were 41 pianos, each one hand-painted by an artist from the participating countries. They were then placed out on the street to be played by passers-by.

I had deep misgivings about this venture. After all, I had spent my entire career telling people to care for their pianos, keep them in an stable environment, and away from abuse - especially things like fists and spilled liquids.

However, out on to the streets they went. Into parks, and plazas, inside subway stations, and outside shops; played by musicians and non-musicians alike, as well as drunken bar patrons, rambunctious teens, and more than a few residents of the city streets.

For the most part, they stayed playable for the duration of the event. There were a couple of instances of vandalism, easily repaired, and more than a few all-out onslaughts by Mother Nature.

I learned a few new things through the experience. For example: pianos are much hardier than I gave them credit for. People are kinder, and more careful with the instruments than I thought they would be, and wherever I went, people were very interested in what I do.

Most surprisingly, the oldest of the pianos seemed to survive better than the newest. Two of the forty-one were over one hundred years old, and although I did have to glue them together a couple of times, they stayed playing, and stayed in tune.

The newest of the pianos were not only the ones that took the most abuse, but, the ones that I had the hardest time to keep operable. Two of them - Panama, and Cayman Islands - a thirty-five year-old Lesage, and a communist-era East German spinet - were rendered completely unplayable by the first rainstorm. Two days later, after baking in the hot sun, not only were they playable again, but they were still (relatively) in tune.

Most miraculous of all, I saw what I can only describe as piano-love: Spontaneous jam-sessions in the evening, piano lessons given outside, families making a holiday out of a street piano scavenger hunt, street-people guarding them and covering them when it rained, musicians making YouTube videos, and one eight-year-old boy, who blogged about his experiences finding and playing every one.

Most of these pianos, if not all of them, will not be able to survive being brought off the street and dried out. Their glue joints will break, the wood will split, the veneers will peel. So, although it was a successful, rewarding, and enlightening adventure, the moral of the story remains the same one that I have been preaching for thirty-five years: Take care of your piano, have it tuned regularly, and keep it off of the streets.

What are pianos made of?

Wood, cast iron, felt, leather, ivory (shudder), plastic, and glue – but mostly wood: spruce, maple, oak, poplar, medium density fiberboard (MDF), and various exotic hardwood veneers, to be more specific.

Maple is used where something has to be strong. Spruce is used where something has to be either light, or resonant, or both. Oak is used for parts of the case that support great stress, and poplar or MDF is used for the rest of the case parts. Veneers such as walnut and mahogany cover the visible parts of the case.

In order to tell you everything you ever needed to know about pianos, you'll need a crash course in terminology, and a bit of a glossary. I'll try to keep it entertaining, but it is, admittedly, a long and boring list.

Just off the top of my head, using an old

Heintzman upright as an example, a piano can contain well over 8000 individual parts. All of these parts fit into three different categories: the Case, the Back and Belly, and the Action and Keyboard. I've organized this list in these categories, arranged alphabetically for quick reference, and have omitted hundreds of parts that are uninteresting (like screws), and parts that I can't say anything funny about (like hinges).

The Case

Basically, this is the part of the piano that you see. However, there are hidden parts to it. The case consists of not only the cabinet parts, but everything that holds all the other parts in place.

Bottom Board: The board at the bottom of the piano, hence the name. Its main function is to hold the mechanism for the pedal action.

Castors: The wheels. Not actually designed for wheeling. In most old pianos, they are designed to chew up hardwood floors.

Cheek Blocks: Sometimes just referred to as cheeks. If you think of the keys as being the "teeth" of the piano, then this is self-explanatory.

Damper Pedal: The right-hand pedal. Pressing this causes the notes to sustain. Also called a (surprise) Sustain Pedal.

Damper Pedal Lever: You press a pedal down, and inside the piano, a lever is levered.

Damper Pedal Spring: Once you stop pressing the pedal, the spring pushes the pedal back up.

Damper Rod: What the other end of the Damper Pedal Lever pushes up. (You'll find out what the rod pushes later.)

Fallboard Back Half: The Fallboard is also called a Key Cover. (It really should by called a Keys Cover, but never mind.) It's held in place by the Cheek Blocks.

Fallboard Front Half: The part of the Fallboard that falls over the keys, and sometimes on your fingers. Also called a Nameboard because the builders have stenciled their names onto it, much like graffiti. (Or, in this case, graffito - a singular mark which identifies the graffitist.) FACT: The finisher who applied the stencil is not called a graffitiationist.

Fallboard Lock: If you don't have a key, don't call a locksmith. In most old pianos, there's just a little triangle inside that can be turned with a small screwdriver, but don't bother - it's essentially useless. A piano should be played, not locked.

Front Board: The large rectangular board above the keyboard. It doubles as a music stand in most old uprights, moving forward when you open the fallboard.

Front Half Lid: This is the part of the lid that opens. In many pianos, the lid is in one piece. This means that it is heavier, and when open, has to lean against the wall behind the piano to stay open during tuning. A tip of the front half of my hat to lids split in two!

Gable: The side of the case.

Gable Wing: The extension on the middle of the gable to which the Keybed is attached.

Hammer Rail Lift Pedal: Usually the left pedal. Also called (erroneously) a Soft Pedal. It moves all the hammers forward, allowing you to use less force to play softly.

Keybed: The case part that supports the Keyboard. It's actually removable by a technician, allowing the piano to turn sharp corners.

Keyslip: The long piece of wood directly in front of the white keys. Its main purpose (other than aesthetics) is to collect pennies which then rub against the keys and make them stick down.

Kick Board: The removable board that your kids kick with their feet because they can't reach the pedals. It covers the bottom part of the inside of the piano, including the mechanism for the pedals, and is a great place to hide things behind.

Kick Board Clasp: A little spring that holds the kick board closed. (Don't show the kids.)

Toe Blocks: The extensions glued onto the bottom of the gable that prevent the piano from falling over on top of you. Bless them! SCIENCE FACT: pianos have two toes, much like a sloth. This might explain why they are so hard to move.

Music Shelf: Usually attached to the bottom edge of the Front Board, it's not so much removable as break-off-able.

Nameboard Felt: A strip of felt glued onto the bottom of the Nameboard (Fallboard), because it looks fancy.

Sostenuto Pedal: The middle pedal in some Heintzman uprights and most grand pianos, this pedal will sustain only the notes that are depressed when you use it. Maybe it will cheer them up.

Trapwork Screws: "Trapwork" is another name for the pedal action. Trivia: The name "Trapwork" comes from Pipe Organ nomenclature. In large organs with a mechanical action, the area in the bottom of the console (keyboard) area is filled with a mechanism that resembles a trap.

Back and Belly

The Back and Belly is the back of the piano (obviously), but also everything attached to the front of the back, like the strings.

Action Hanger Bolts: The bolts from which the action hangs.

Anchor Pins: Piano strings have two ends. One end is attached to a pin that turns, the other to a pin that does not. The string is therefore "anchored" to this pin.

Backing Plate: A maple board that stretches across the top and back of an upright piano.

Bass Bridge Body: The strings vibrate, and the soundboard amplifies this vibration so you can hear it. The bridges connect the string to the soundboard. They not only act as a bridge, they kind of look like one, too.

Bridge Screw Buttons: Also called soundboard buttons, these are large wooden washers that look like, well, buttons.

Bridge Pins: There are almost five hundred of these little steel pins. They guide the strings across the bridge. Even though they are small, they are mighty, AND mightily important. If they weren't there, the piano would sound like a snare drum.

Capo D'Astro Bar: The strings are forced, under pressure, to pass under this bar. Kind of like doing the limbo - something performed in other bars, under peer pressure.

Capo D'Astro Screws: These screws hold the bar down, kind of like bouncers.

Lifting Handles: These handles on the back of the piano are used by PROFESSIONAL PIANO MOVERS to lift the piano onto a dolly. (Note the caps.)

Music Wire: This is what the Strings are made of, so in fact they should be called wires, not strings. But, c'est la vie. If all musical family groups were named after their source materials, string players would be called "Catgutters", brass players, "Alloyists", and the woodwinds would be "Bamboozers".

Nose Bolts: The nose bolts support the plate in the middle of the soundboard. They stick out through the board, are long, pointy, and have a weird shape near the end. (Kind of like Pinocchio's after a boxing match.)

Nose Bolt Nuts: A lot of piano parts are named after parts of the body... never mind.

Pinblock: The block of wood that holds the tuning pins tight. If this cracks, separates, warps, gets wet, or dries out, it has to be replaced. Luckily, this doesn't happen often. It's a big job.

Plate: This is the large cast iron metal thing that's painted gold. It's also called a harp. Harpo Marx played one once, got a big laugh, and then a hernia operation – it's the heaviest part of the piano!

Plate Screws: These are really big screws that hold the back together. Without them, the piano would be, well, screwed.

Posts: The large tall wooden beams on the back of the piano.

Spacers, Lower: The spacers space out the posts. Spacepost? Beam me up, Scotty.

Spacers, Upper: Longer than the Lower Spacers, the Upper Spacers also support the Backing Plate, which supports the Pinblock, which supports the... you get the picture.

Strings, Bass: Basically, the lowest strings in the piano. They are usually wound with copper, although other materials have been tried in the past.

Strings, Treble: The upper strings. Plain wire strings, they are jealous of the fancier bass strings which pass over them. They overcompensate by outnumbering the bass strings three to one.

Stringing Braid: A part of the string is made to sing, the other part is mute. The stringing braid goes through this part, it's red and fancy – a beaut!

Treble Bridge Body: The next listed part sits on top of this part.

Treble Bridge Cap: The previous part sits under this part. Remember the Bridge Pins? This is the piece of wood that holds those pins tight. If it doesn't, the strings will buzz when excited.

Tuning Pins (244 of them): "Hey!" (I hear you ask) "88 keys, but 244 pins?" Yup. Each treble note uses three strings. The lower bass one per note, the upper bass – two.

Action and Keyboard

If the Action is the engine of the piano, then the Keyboard is the control panel.

Action Capstans: These capstans hold the bottom of the Action Brackets, just as Action Hanger Bolts hold the top. Salty Trivia: The name "Capstan" is a nautical term. It's basically a vertical windlass, which has nothing to do with the piano version, except both can turn if needed.

Action Rail: The rail onto which all the action parts are screwed.

Butts: More physiological nomenclature. More on this later.

Butt Leather: Don't get me started.

Back Check Heads: The Back Checks catch the Butts so that the Hammers don't bobble against the string making a sound like a zither.

Balance Rail: The keys are basically like little teeter-totters, and they balance on the Balance Rail.

Balance Rail Bushings: These little cushions hold the key, preventing them from wobbling like Weebles.

Balance Rail Paper Punchings: These are little paper washers that come in different thicknesses and are colour coded for easy reference. Technicians use these to adjust how high a key sits when it's at rest.

Balance Rail Pins: The pin in the middle of each key.

Balance Rail Punchings: Little felt donuts that sit on top of the Paper Punchings and directly under the middle of the key. Mmm, donuts.

Capstan Heads: More Capstans – 88 more in fact. These are the adjustable connections between the keys and the action.

Catches: The Catches are the parts that the Backchecks catch, when the Backchecks have caught Butts. (Say that five times fast.)

Centre Pins: Almost every moving part in the action rotates on these little silver-plated brass pins.

Centre Pin Bushings: The sleeves in which the Centre Pins sit and spin.

Dampers: Dampers stop the strings from ringing. It's a piano tuner's joke that they are called this, because when they don't work right, the piano makes that damn purr.

Damper Bodies: Seriously, don't get me started.

Damper Spoons: These lift the bottom of the dampers, and are shaped like forks. (Just kidding.)

Front Rail: When your finger pushes down a key, it stops because it hits this rail.

Front Rail Bushings: Like the Balance Rail bushing, except under the front of each key.

Front Rail Paper Punchings: Just like the Balance Rail Paper Punchings, except bigger donuts. Mmm, bigger donuts.

Front Rail Pins: The front of the keys are guided by these pins as they descend.

Front Rail Punchings: These little felt donuts sit between the key and the rail so that it doesn't make a horrible clacking sound when you play.

Hammers: The things that hit the strings.

Hammer Rest Rail: The rail against which the Hammers rest.

Hammer Shanks: The sticks to which the hammers are glued.

Heads, Ivory: Elephants were slaughtered horribly and in great numbers just to make these key tops. I am grateful that its now outlawed. Plastic is now most commonly used, although it is possible to get faux-ivory made from cow bone. No joke here. Sorry.

Jacks: Remember the Butts? The Hammers are glued to Shanks, the Shanks are glued to Butts, and the Jacks kick the Butts so that the Hammers hit the Strings.

Jack Flanges: In a piano, a flange is a part that holds the axis point for every moving part. This makes it different from what the rest of the world thinks of as a flange. Perhaps it should be spelled "Phalange"? No bones about it: Spelled that way, flange looks fancy!

Jack Slap Rails: I'm not telling you what these are for, but suffice it to say, they are the Piano's appendix.

Jack Springs: If these little coil springs weaken or break, the key will not work - period. As Stanislavsky famously said, "There are no small parts, only small actors." These small parts play a big role in upright piano actions.

Key Bodies: Also called Key Sticks, but that sounds a little annoying.

Key Fronts, Celluloid: Even though they spared no expense (and no elephants) to make the ivory tops, they cheapened out a bit by covering the front facing edge of the white keys with the earliest form of plastic. Useless Trivia: Celluloid was originally called Xylonite, but they changed the name so that Superman wouldn't be confused and fear wooden glockenspiels. Further Useless Trivia: "Glockenspiel" is German for "Bells-Play". (It's a good thing the Italians named the piano, or I'd be writing a book about Musikstahldrahtspiels.)

Let-off Buttons: To stop the Jacks from kicking the Butts all the way into the Strings, the Let-off Buttons stop them part-way.

Let-off Screws: These are actually adjustment screws, not merely inclined planes wrapped helicaly around a vertical axis.

Regulation Rail: The rail that holds the Let-off Buttons and Screws.

Sharps: The politically correct name for the Black Keys. You could call them "Flats", but then British people would want to live in them.

Sostenuto Rail Monkey: In a grand piano, the Monkey is a little dowel that grabs onto a little bar and swings – hence the name. In an upright, it's a bent piece of brass. It's still called a monkey, though, because it's cute.

Tails, Ivory: The Ivories are in two parts - Heads or Tails. It's a toss-up as to which is bigger, as one is wider, and the other longer, but it's a sure bet that either way, the elephants lost.

Whippen Bodies: The Whippens are the parts of the action that hold the Jacks. Now you know how the action works: The Keys are teeter-totters. You press the front, the back rises, the Capstans lift the Whippens, making the Jacks kick the Butts, which makes the Hammers hit the Strings.

Whippen Heel Cloth: The Heel is the contact point between the Whippen and the Capstan. The aforementioned cloth is actually a thin, but tightly-woven piece of felt.

Hinges: There once was a man made with hinges, who when bending, would feel certain twinges. He did rattle and squeak, 'till with oil he did tweak, now indulges in lubricant binges.

(Sorry about that. I just couldn't resist.)

How are pianos made?

Now you know every part of the piano. But, how are they built? I'll try to outline the process in a simple way, but keep in mind that building a good piano is anything but. Not only do you have to make an instrument that plays in the way people expect, but also something that looks nice, and, most importantly, sounds nice.

Building a piano not only involves skill in

woodworking, but also math and physics. A slight miscalculation can result in a piano not only having poor tone, but also playing poorly, and prematurely aging. Poor craftsmanship not only results in flaws that you can't see, but flaws that can have severe effects on every aspect of its playability and serviceability.

The most common problem in modern piano building is the lack of time and resources spent on the instrument. It's ironic, but older pianos, though well built, were often poorly designed. New pianos, though usually well designed are, far too often, poorly built.

There are four distinct parts to the process: The Back & Belly, The Action and Keyboard, The Case and Finishing, and The Final Assembly. The first three things happen at once, and all come together for the fourth. I will describe them separately, based on factory divisions.

First, the "raw" materials arrive at the factory. When I say raw, I don't mean actually mean "raw". A lot of the parts arrive in various states of... "cookedness".

Most of the wood arrives in rough cut form from a sawmill. The wood is sorted for its various uses, and undergoes different techniques of drying, depending on their eventual use.

The plates arrive from a foundry in various

degrees of completion. They are often set aside to season for a while like the wood, because, believe it or not, the plates change in shape and size for many months after they are cast. Some companies season their plates for years!

In general, most modern piano makers buy the actions and keyboards ready-made from companies such as Renner, and Kluge. However, they generally arrive unassembled.

Felt, leather, and other materials arrive in bulk, and are usually cut as needed, although it is not unusual for a lot of this work to have been done by the suppliers.

The following describes the traditional method of building an upright piano:

The Back and Belly

Using detailed drawings and pre-made jigs and machines, the backs are assembled en masse for each model and set aside and stored for later use. They are basically just a series of large posts, separated by spacer blocks. At the top of the back, where the pinblock will be, the spacers are larger, and are faced with a thick rectangular board called a backing plate, that is set into the sides of the pillars. The pinblock will eventually be attached to it, so it is very firmly set into the back. After all, it will soon be supporting tons of stress – and I mean tons!

In old-timey piano factories, the guys who made the soundboard were called "Belly-MEN". In modern factories, this term is no longer used in order to not insult Santa Claus.

The soundboard builders hand-select the spruce that is to be used, sort it into different collections depending on grains-per-inch, machine-plane them into the rough thicknesses, and cut them to approximate lengths. (Slow-growth spruce have closer grains, fast-growth spruce have wider grains.)

The boards are then laid out on a large table into the rough shape of the finished board. They use different qualities of wood for different parts of the soundboard, as sound travels in different patterns based on frequency. Typically, the closest grained wood is used in the top treble, and the grain can become coarser towards the bass.

(There are certain parts of the soundboard which actually vibrate very little, and not only do piano makers often use fast growth spruce, but sometimes, they are even segregated from the rest of the board using a kind of sound-dam – a piece of maple glued across the two sections.)

The board blank is then cut using a pattern into the desired shape, and placed either onto a table with a convex shape called a Belly-Table, or a series of slightly curved clamps. The ribs are put into place on the board, and then glued together. The ribs are all slightly bowed so that the soundboard has a convex shape.

The old-fashioned Belly-Table is actually quite a cool little rig. It's a large wooden table that has a working surface that is convex, and a "roof" above it that is strongly reinforced. It kind of looks like a really large and uncomfortable bunk-bed. The soundboard lies on the bottom bunk, and the ribs are clamped to the board by using many sticks of wood called "go-bars" which are bent into place between the bottom of the upper bunk and the soundboard below.

After the ribs are attached, the bridge is glued and screwed onto the board and positioned using a special jig. In most factories, the bridge is pre-notched and pinned, and has a concave shape to match the soundboard.

The soundboard is convex so that when the strings press down onto the bridge, the soundboard is under tension. It's kind of like a drum head - tightly fastened around the perimeter and taut. In fact, you can play an unstrung soundboard like a drum, and the sound it makes is like a large tom-tom!

The completed soundboard then has a frame glued around its perimeter, and is glued onto the back. The edges of the board are flush to the edge of the frame and the back. When the sides of the piano are glued on, the soundboard cannot expand in any direction other than in and out; in other words, the direction the vibrations of the strings create.

The pinblock blank (a kiln-dried sheet of laminated maple) is then glued onto the backing plate and kept in position by dowels and many large clamps. The plate is then lowered onto the assembled back, and its support structure is assembled. The nose-bolt holes, plate-screw holes and tuning-pin holes are marked and drilled.

The tuning-pin holes are drilled at a slight angle (6-8 degrees) using a special drill-press that keeps this angle while moving on a large reticulated arm. When all the holes are drilled, the back is then strung, tuned using a felt pick (chip-tuning), and then the case is attached.

The Action and Keyboard

In another part of the factory, the action and keyboard are being prepared. The rails are made and drilled, and the frames are attached. They are then put on a rotating cradle, and the whippens, butts and damper bodies are screwed into position.

The key frames are made, drilled and felted, the guide pins are inserted, and the keys are cut, drilled, pre-weighted, and placed on the frame.

Much of the assembly of the action and the final weighting and adjustment of the keys is left unfinished until the piano has been assembled, and the action and keyboard have been installed into the finished piano.

The Case and Finishing

Most of the case parts are made and finished in pieces. The gables and gable-ends (the sides of the piano) are glued and clamped onto the finished back. The rest of the case, including the keybed, is then assembled. At this point, the piano moves onto the last part of the process – the part where the magic happens.

Final Assembly

This stage is much, much more than putting everything together. This is the part in the process where the piano is literally brought to life. In the old factories, the men who did this job were called "Fly-Finishers". This was partly because they moved from one piano to the next (flying from one piano to another), and also because things seemed to happen quickly: A piano would arrive literally in pieces, unrecognizable as an instrument, and by the end of the day, it would all come together.

My grandfather was a fly-finisher at the Martin-Orme factory in Ottawa, and my father often told me that it was these "end-of-the-line" technicians that were the secret behind making a great piano.

They installed the incomplete action, bent the damper wires to the correct shape, installed the damper heads and dampers, and gave them an initial regulation.

The hammer shanks were cut, the hammer heads installed and aligned, and then the keyboard was installed. At this point, a quick regulation would make the piano play for the first time.

The piano would then be rolled into a quiet

room, and after the glue had set overnight, it would be given a series of tunings, finely regulated and voiced.

In some factories, the piano would be played-in by a machine before the final regulation and voicing.

After the piano has been completed, it is given a final spit and polish, and then sent to another part of the factory where it is crated, loaded onto trucks, shipped across oceans, back onto a truck and placed onto the sales floor of your friendly neighbourhood piano store.

Building a grand is a similar process, but a lot more involved. For instance, the back of the piano is integrated with the case, and is built at the same time.

The curved shape of a grand piano is made (in most factories) by bending sheets of wood around a form where it is pressed into the familiar shape of a grand. There are actually two parts to this; an outer rim (the outside of which you see), and the inner rim (which you can only see if you look underneath). The outer rim often has exotic veneer facing both sides. The inner rim is the bed of the soundboard, and has the posts notched into it for strength.

The process of building the soundboard in a grand is basically the same for the upright, however, installing it is an entirely different process. The soundboard is carefully shaped so that it fits very tightly to the inside of the outer rim, and the top of the inner rim is notched so that the ends of the ribs are also tight to the rim.

The soundboard is then heated in a hot-box until the moisture content of the board is below the average lowest humidity of the area where it will be eventually be living. While the board is still warm, it is quickly glued and clamped into place.

As the board cools and absorbs the humidity in the air, it expands slightly. However, like in an upright, it can't expand outward. This creates that all-important tension needed for the board to be resonant.

How does a piano work?

You press a key, and a note sounds. In a nutshell, here's how an upright works: Pressing the key down lifts the back of the key up. This raises the whippen, forcing the jack to tilt the hammer mechanism toward the string. Halfway toward the string, a spoon on the back of the whippen lifts the damper off the string, and just before it hits, the force on the hammer is removed when the jack is tripped out from underneath the butt. When you let go of the key, everything in the action returns to its original position because of springs.

After the string has been struck by the hammer, it vibrates across its entire length in a sine-wave. This vibration is transferred to the soundboard through the bridge, and the soundboard, like a speaker, amplifies it so that you can hear the sound loud and clear.

A grand works in a different way. This is because instead of using a spring to return the action to a reset position, it uses gravity. There is also an extra part to the whippen called a "repetition lever" which resets the jack so quickly that you can play the note again, without having to return the key to the fully "up" position. This allows for a much faster repeat, and is one of the main benefits of a grand over an upright.

Because it uses gravity instead of springs, the touch is more consistent. Also, because of the repetition lever, each key has a noticeable little click that you can feel near the bottom of the key stroke. You can feel it, but you can't hear it. Good pianists can use this to increase the accuracy of their touch.

That was the nutshell. Now, here's the meat: Every moving part in a piano is adjustable to a certain extent. Some have adjustment mechanisms built in, others are made to tolerances that can only be changed using very specialized tools.

There is a roughly universal value to some of

the movements of the action parts, however they can differ from piano to piano, and from make to make. How high a key sits, for example, is based on having a small gap between the top of the keytop tail, and the bottom of the fallboard. However, wood warps and wears, so the height is adjustable by using small paper washers of different thicknesses underneath the fulcrum of the key.

How far it depresses is also (relatively) standard, but the felt washer underneath the key not only can vary slightly in thickness, but it compresses. Therefore, paper washers underneath that felt front rail punching regulate the "dip" of the key to the desired amount.

The key body is weighted with small lead weights to not only ensure that the key has a certain amount of resistance, but to also ensure that it will return quickly to the rest position quickly. These weights are installed in the factory, and although they can be removed or repositioned, it is a complicated process which should only be performed by a technician specifically trained to weight keys.

At the back of the key, an adjustable capstan "connects" the key to the action. If it is too low, there is space between the jack and the butt which creates "lost-motion". If the capstan is too high, the jack won't reset underneath the butt.

There are adjustments all through the action like this, and although some tolerances can be reasonably large (such as spring tension), most have to be finely adjusted or the action will not play the way it was intended.

The overall geometry of the action is set during the design and building stage, and changing any of these measurements can literally make the piano unplayable. For example, the hammers must hit the string at a very precise point in its length, and a very precise point on the hammer itself. If these are altered even a fraction of an inch, the tone of the piano will be negatively affected.

Even a seemingly small thing like altering the size of the whippen heel by a few millimetres can change the weight of the key from normal to unbearably heavy.

Like the action, the tolerances and adjustments of the back and belly are many, varied, and critical. In order for a single string to have the correct tone, it must be exactly the right length, tension, and thickness. All these measurements must be in balance not only for that one string, but across all 240+ strings.

If you have to have a shorter string for the same note in a smaller piano, you have to increase the thickness, and this can negatively affect the tone – likewise if you increase or decrease the tension, as well.

If there is too much tension in one part of the back, that area could go out of tune faster than the rest of the strings. As you can see, getting all of these things (called "scaling") right is complicated and critical.

Each string is under a lot of tension – ranging from 120 to 160 pounds per inch. Across the whole scale, that adds up to 14 to 16 tons of pressure. That's enough force to tear a two-car garage off of its foundation, and because of this, not only does the plate and the back have to be very strong, it has to be designed to hold that tension, and more.

Each string is held in place, and up to tension, by the tuning pin on one end, and by the anchor pin on the other end. A few (very terrible) manufacturers experimented with having anchor pins being cast into the plate. They soon found out that they could break off during stringing, shooting the pin like a bullet toward the stringer.

The tuning pin has to be tight enough so that it will hold the tension, but loose enough to be able to turn, enabling the string to be tuned. The pin has to be on a slight angle and set at a certain depth so that as the string is wrapped around the pin, it makes a neat, tight wrap, and doesn't wrap on top of itself.

The point at which the string interacts with the bridge is so critical, that not only does it have to be at an exact point on each string, it has to be at an exact height. An error in these measurements can not only ruin the piano's tone, but its ability to sustain the tone, as well.

A Brief History of pianos

"Daddy, where do pianos come from?"

"Well, my child, when a harpsichord and a clavichord really love each other..."

Like most inventions, the piano grew out of improvements upon earlier instruments. The lyre inspired the harp, the harp inspired the harpsichord, the harpsichord inspired the clavichord, and at the beginning of the eighteenth century, these instruments inspired three men in three different countries to invent the precursor of the piano. They were experimenting on exactly the same idea at roughly the same time. It is said that they were not aware of each other's efforts, and that very well might be true. Perhaps it was simply that the time had come for this particular scientific and cultural advancement.

Jean Marius of Paris, Christoph Gottlieb Schröter of Vienna, and Bartolomeo Christofori of

Padua were all trying to improve upon the harpsichord, which was the most popular keyboard instrument of their time. While each of them succeeded in improving the playing mechanism of the instrument, one of them, Bartolomeo Christofori, went further. He ended up creating an entirely new instrument altogether which he called, unimaginatively: "Piano e Forte"- Soft and Loud. Luckily for us tuners, the name over the years shortened to simply "Piano", or we would all be deaf.

In 1745 C.E. Friedeici, an organ builder, solved the problem of the piano's enormously long case by building one in an upright shape. However, it was now enormously high, and therefore could be dangerous if played in a strong wind. He went on to build one in a rectangular shape, with the keyboard placed on one of the longer sides. Because musicians are notoriously bad at geometry, it was called a "Square" piano. The idea caught on, and then spread throughout Europe.

In 1781, Broadwood of England started a revolution with a relatively simple idea. In order to understand the significance of his innovation, remember that a piano string has two ends - one fixed at what is called the "Anchor Pin", and the other turned around an iron pin hammered tightly into a layered block of maple called a pinblock. The square pianos up to this time had the pinblock on the side, and the shortest string (the highest note) had a short key to play it. The longest string (near the back of the instrument) had a long key on the left hand. This made the touch uneven, a problem Broadwood corrected by placing the block at the rear of the instrument. Now the hammers all rose directly from the back of the key, and the touch was significantly improved. It was further discovered that two things could radically alter the tone: the shape of the soundboard, and the positioning of the hammer in relation to the string.

All the piano makers of the time, upon seeing and hearing the Broadwood instrument, stole his ideas and ran with them. Or, as we say in the business: "They started to experiment with these advancements."

The next evolution in the piano came in America in 1825 when Alpheus Babcock invented an iron frame to stabilize the piano so that it would stay in tune. However, it was Jonas Chickering of Boston who got the eventual credit for this invention, for twelve years later, he used it to increase the piano's power, using heavier strings, and was awarded a patent in 1840.

Henry Engelhardt Steinway, and his famous company, Steinway & Sons, are generally credited with some of the most important improvements in the construction of pianos after the 1850's. Steinway introduced the idea of crossing the bass strings over the treble strings, for instance, to permit a smaller size, a development referred to as "The Overstrung Scale". Never mind the fact that, like the iron frame, it was originally invented by Babcock.

They went on to improve the soundboard as an acoustic amplifier, and to improve the bridges, the pinblock, and the piano's' action. Almost all of Steinway's improvements to the piano happened before the twentieth century. Most of their attempts at improving the piano since then have been minor, or in some cases, such as the use of Teflon action bushings between 1962 and 1981, disasters. Other than that, the modern Steinway grand has remained basically unchanged since the 1920's.

Steinway's influence over the North American piano market has been considerable; most people know the name Steinway even if they nothing about pianos at all. This is the result of three remarkably astute decisions made in the late 1800's: First of all, it was decided that instead of standardizing their touch weight and depth to that of the other pianos, they made their keys very slightly heavier to play, and very slightly shallower. Secondly, they opened their own Concert Hall (featuring their own pianos) which was the home of the New York Philharmonic until the opening of Carnegie Hall in 1891. The result of these two decisions was that the public saw the Steinway in performance exclusively, and performers bought Steinway's themselves so that they would be accustomed to the different touch. Today, new concert venues, when shopping for pianos, are often astounded that the Steinway concert grands are among the least expensive on the market. This third astute decision ensures that Steinway stays in the forefront of the public eye.

D.H. Baldwin, a music teacher from Cincinnati, Ohio, gradually moved into the clan of piano builders by first selling the instruments, then by hiring people to build pump organs, and finally by making pianos. Baldwin was much more interested in doing God's work than his own, however, and left the company in the hands of two men, Lucien Wulsin and George Armstrong, Jr. The two men took the company from ashes to riches, struggling under the financial burden left to them by Baldwin when he bequeathed all his assets to the church. Eventually, with the help of some very talented artisans, they managed to unify five poor divisions of the company into one, and then to produce decent grand pianos and passable uprights. Interestingly, the Baldwin company inadvertently advertised the fact that they were not as pleased with their uprights as they should have been - the name Baldwin was not stamped on a single upright until well after the Second World War. Baldwin's stock in the public eye went up considerably due to the exposure given to them by Wladziu Valentino Liberace. On television in the 1950's and 1960's, and in Las Vegas in the 1970's and 1980's, the "Baldwin" name was easily visible on all of his customized pianos.

Theodore Heintzman, an expatriate German like Steinway, succeeded in building what was at the time the ultimate upright piano, but still within the price range of most families. He had shared a workbench with Henry Steinway when they were both apprentices in the "old country". Henry immigrated to New York, Theodore to Toronto, Canada. For a while, in the early years, it was a toss-up as to who would become the pre-eminent builder. Steinway ended up winning by a landslide because of his grands, and because he choose the right country in which to become rich and famous. Poor Heintzman, and the company he left behind, struggled mightily against the forces of a disorganized country, a belligerent government, a struggling economy, and the flood of cheap pianos from Japan. Eventually, in 1985, they lost the battle. The Heintzman uprights of the 1920's, the greatest upright pianos ever produced anywhere in the world, are becoming fewer and fewer as time marches on. There will never be another true Heintzman. The company was mortally wounded in the 1960's by exceedingly poor management, and killed in the 1970's by poor government.

The next dramatic step in the evolution of the piano came during the last four decades; however, it was mostly about manufacturing processes and marketing, and not about moving the instrument on to the next level. The Japanese piano maker, Yamaha, changed the way pianos have been traditionally built, much in the same way Henry Ford changed the car industry. Yamaha perfected the mass production of pianos. Other makers struggled to catch up and produce them in large quantities, but only Yamaha managed to do it and still turn out a decent product. Their secret was the training of the technicians at the "end of the line". Yamaha's factory technicians are trained to "set up" the pianos after production to such an extent that they are very stable and playable right out of the box. This makes them an easy sell compared to most other "economy" makes, which need dealer service to make them sellable.

The Kawai factory in Japan is but a hop, skip, and a jump away from Yamaha's, and operated as a rival sibling for many years. They became a major manufacturer in their own right by building "Howard" pianos for Baldwin. As these pianos increased their earnings, Kawai disassociated themselves from Baldwin, and started to build and sell pianos under their own name. Yamaha and Kawai changed the entire landscape of the piano industry in the 1970's by building pianos that were both good and affordable at the same time.

At one time, a small builder could grow slowly and build quality instruments with in-house craftsmen. Now, because of global sales, when a company gets big, they expand to the regions where the labour is the cheapest. Eventually, these regions produce quality products, their prices rise, and the production of pianos is shifted to the next low-cost area.

Yamaha now makes pianos in many different factories in many parts of the world, including China, Indonesia, and the United States. Of course, Yamaha makes many things other than pianos. One area in which they have excelled, but yet is little known to the general public, is the design and manufacture of robots and robotic systems. This fact segues into my last point about piano evolution: Once upon a time, all pianos were made by hand by a few talented craftsmen. Today, this tradition still exists in but a handful of piano companies such as Bechstein, Blüthner,

Bösendorfer, Steingraeber and Steinway. Yamaha's gift to the piano world is to have made craftsman-made pianos from small shops few and far-between, and entry-level, cookie-cutter instruments from large factories a dime-a-dozen, and disposable. In the "Golden Era" of the piano, when they were all hand-made, they were a luxury item equal in cost then, as buying a new car is now, but built to last a lifetime.

Not all mass-produced pianos are created equal, however. There will always be subtle differences between individual pianos from a single production line because they are made chiefly out of organic materials that have unique individual properties. The greatest difference between mass-produced pianos, however, lies in the individual philosophy of the builders. With few exceptions, piano builders are proud of what they do, and believe that they are striving toward a good product. However, there is a huge range of quality available, and for the most part it is evidenced by the price. There are very good reasons why some pianos are cheap, and some are expensive. With a few exceptions, a piano's price is the best indication of its quality.

Who Builds pianos?

During the past three centuries, literally thousands of brand names have come and gone. Some names still survive, either as original builders or as an adopted name for a line of pianos from a "new" builder. In the following list, I have tried to include the dates of the builders. In some cases, such as "Boston", the builders have not stated the date of formation, possibly to obfuscate the fact that the piano is relatively new. Please note that the dates supplied below may refer to either the current manufacturer or the original manufacturers, depending on which list the name is included.

When searching for information on a specific piano, try to ascertain its age. This can be obtained in most cases by finding the serial number (stamped or painted onto the top of the piano's plate) and the make, and then you can look up its approximate age by going online and pointing your browser to: www.bluebookofpianos.com

Current Builders

During the "Golden Age" of the piano (1880-1929), many builders made three lines of pianos: Their "A" line, ex. "Mason & Risch"; their "B" line, ex. "Henry Herbert"; and a "C" line, which could have any name on it a retailer could request (as long as the name wasn't already trademarked). This tradition remains to this day. There are many, many new piano brands which do not relate to an existing manufacturer. Having said this, it should be noted that many current builders are not included in this list.

Baldwin (1890 -) Bought by Gibson Guitar Company in 2004. Liberace's favourite piano.

Bechstein (1853 -) - Exceptionally fine pianos from Berlin, Germany. One of Carl Bechstein's descendants, Helene, was an ardent admirer of Adolf Hitler. She bought him a Mercedes and let him use her summer home. In return, he almost destroyed her country. Not a fair trade.

Bluthner (1853 -) Also exceptionally fine pianos from Leipzig, Germany. (1853 was a good year for starting a piano company!)

Bösendorfer (1828 -) Made in Vienna, Austria. Bösendorfer is a big name in pianos, with some BIG pianos to its name, including the famous Imperial grand – 10 feet of piano, and featuring 97 keys instead of the normal, boring old 88. From 1966 to 2002, it was owned by The Jasper Corporation, also known as Kimball International. German owned from 2002 - 2007, now owned by Yamaha. One of my all-time favourite piano makers, I own, and often wear, a Bösendorfer baseball cap. (I mention this in case they want to give me money in return for promoting them. Hint, hint.).

Boston - (? -) A Division of Steinway & Sons. Steinway designed, built by Kawai.

Chickering & Sons (1823 -) Sold to Aeolian in the 1930's, then sold to Wurlitzer in the 1990's. Built by Samick for a while. Now owned by Baldwin.

Dongbei (? -) Chinese manufacturer of many brands. Recently purchased by Gibson (who also own Baldwin).

Fazioli - (1978 -) Paolo Fazioli set out to make the finest piano in the world. Now just over 25 years later, many say he succeeded. I visited the Fazioli factory in 2004, and for a special treat, was driven at high speed by Paolo in his BMW to the Val di Fiemme Forest. Once there, he showed me the grove of trees that were the genetic decendants of the trees used by Stradivarius for his famous violins. At large tree, Paolo knocked on it as if it was a door that he expected to open. I asked him if that was a special method for testing the tree. He said: "No, I am just saying hello." He's a crazy genius, much like an Italian Einstein. He kind of looks like Einstein, too!

Feurich (1851 -) One of the first European makers of the upright piano.

Guangzhou / Pearl River (1956 -) Chinese manufacturer of many brands, including Yamaha.

Hazelton Bros. - (2003 -) Made by The Samick Music Corporation (SMC)

Heintzman - (1989 -) Not the Canadian original, but the Chinese up-and-comer.

Ibach (1794 -) For over 200 years, fine German pianos. (They also made pipe organs until 1906.)

Kawai (1927 -) The "other" Japanese piano.

Kemble (1917 -) Not to be confused with Kimball. The best-selling British piano in the world, they are now made by Yamaha. They are a kind of hybrid, part English, part Japanese. (Kind of like Sean Lennon, except with strings attached.)

Knabe (2003 -) Now made by SMC, Knabe is a very old and respected name in American pianos.

Kohler & Campbell (2003 -) Now made by Samick (SMC).

Mason & Hamlin (1996 -) Now owned by Pianodisc, one of the finest pianos currently made in North America. (Which isn't saying much.)

Petrof (1864 -) Czech it out!

Samick (2003 -) Now operating under the name SMC Music, they are one of the largest piano builders in the world, and make many lines of pianos, some under the names of former great American builders such as Kohler & Campbell, Sohmer, and Knabe.

Sauter (1819 -)

Schimmel (1885 -) Truly the most advanced piano in the world, and in my humble opinion, one of the finest makers in the world today.

Seiler (1849 -) Is there such a thing as a perfect piano? Seiler says they are trying to find out, at least.

Sohmer (2003 -) Now made by Samick (SMC), Sohmer is, like Knabe, a very old and respected name in American pianos.

Steingraeber & Sohne (1852 -) Possibly the most unusual piano factory in the world, partly because, aside from some modern machinery, their pianos are built the old fashioned way – by a relatively small number of craftsmen.

Steinway (1853 -) In their own words, the "Instrument of the Immortals". Unfortunately, many of those immortals are now deceased. However, Steinway is still the most selected concert piano in the world.

Yamaha (1887 -) My father was one of the first Canadian Dealers of Yamaha pianos. He had to convince those early customers that the Japanese knew what they were doing. Imagine that now!

Past Builders

This is a partial list, containing only the names of relatively common builders, or those that have historical significance.

Acrosonic - A division of Baldwin

Aeolian - (1932 - 1985) Aeolian manufactured pianos under many piano names: Aeolian, Duo Art, Gabler, Stuyvesant, Acoustigrand, Ellsworth, Haines Bros., Pianola, Ampico, Knabe, Foster Armstrong, Laffargue, Stroud, Chickering, Marshall & Wendell, Normandie, Vose, A. A. Chase, Mason & Hamlin, Lindeman, Weber, Franklin, Primatone, Washburn and Wheelock. One of the earliest piano Conglomerate Corporations, Aeolian bought many companies which collapsed during the Depression, and many of their "brand names" still survive today under new ownership.

Bell (1864 - 1925) High-quality pianos made in Guelph, Ontario, Canada. Bought by Lesage pianos in 1934.

Broadwood (1774 - ?) By appointment to her majesty the Queen - the makers of Beethoven's favourite piano. (It was the only one that didn't collapse under his fingers!)

Chickering & Sons (1823 -1932) Bought by Aeolian during the Depression, later sold to Baldwin.

Erard (1800 - 1981?) Famous piano and harp maker. Partnered with Gaveau, and by Schimmel in 1971.

Gaveau (1847 -1981) See Erard.

Gerhard Heintzman (1877 -1927) Made by a nephew of THE Heintzman. Bought by THE Heintzman, and used as a second-line. I have highlighted the THE's because many people mistake G. Heintzman for Heintzman, but, believe me, there's a difference. Before Gerhard Heintzman opened his own company, he worked for Lansdowne, and Nordheimer.

Gourlay, Winter & Leeming (1904 - 1924) Bought by Sherlock-Manning. Discontinued in 1968.

Haines Bros. (1851 - 1942)

Hamilton (1801 - 2000) Made by Baldwin.

Hazelton Bros. (1849 - 1957) Bought by Kohler & Campbell in 1957, the trade name bought by Samick-Bechstein in 2003.

Heintzman & Co. (1870 - 1985) The premier Canadian piano, and one of the best upright piano manufacturers in the world. They made good grands, too, but their uprights were truly wonderful. Bought by Sklar-Pepplar in 1985, sold to The Music Stand, made for a small period of time by Kimball, then made in limited numbers in Eastern Europe. Still Canadian owned, they are now made in China.

Karn (1868 - 1924) At one time, one of the largest builders in Canada. Also made pump organs.

Kimball (1865 - ?) Originally specializing in square pianos, Kimball gradually broadened out to theatre organs, uprights and small grands in the early 20th century. Bought by the Jasper Corp. in 1959, eventually owned by the Habig Corp. who also bought **Bösendorfer.** Made a large number of mass-produced entry-level pianos culminating in providing 100 pianos for the Los Angeles Olympic Games in 1984. Today, Kimball is no longer in the piano business.

Knabe (1837 - present) Originally located in Baltimore, Knabe was once one of Steinway's closest competitors. Bought by Aeolian during the Depression. Now made by Samick Music Corp. in S. Korea.

Kohler & Campbell (1896 - present) Made over fifty different brands of pianos at their New York location which now is in the middle of Central Park. Now made in Indonesia by Samick.

Lesage (1942 - 1981) One of the last Canadian builders. Lesage bought out two other well-known makes Bell and Willis. One of the Lesage family (Jean) was premier of Quebec during the 1960's.

Mason & Hamlin (1865 - present) Made pianos and organs in New York. Bought by Aeolian in 1924, most recently owned by Gary and Kirk Burgett, the founders of Pianodisc.

Mason & Risch (1871 - 1985) Large and well-known Canadian builder of pianos. Bought out by Aeolian. For the last decade or so of its existence, M&R's were built in the U.S. and assembled in Scarborough, ON.

Nordheimer (1840- 1928) A & S Nordheimer started out as a music store, selling other people's pianos. Eventually, they started building their own, and very good ones at that. In 1928, Heintzman bought Nordheimer and used the name for its lower priced instruments. Nordheimer Ravine, in the city of Toronto, is named after them, and marks the path of a stream that used to flow into their estate. Castle Frank Brook was re-routed into an underground pipe in order to build the Toronto Subway System.

Sherlock-Manning (1875 - 1985) The last of the Canadian builders, S-M was run for many years after the Second World War by the Heintzman family. In 1981 it was bought by Draper Brothers Reid, Ltd.

Sohmer (1872-1971) Another of the many New York builders, the name is now owned by Samick.

Steinway (1853-present) The opposite of Heintzman, Steinway is known for their grands, and not so much for their uprights. New Steinways have a distinct smell because of the type (and amount) of lacquer that they use. I grew up with this aroma, and to this day, I love to stop and smell the Steinways.

Weber (1862-1968) Many pianos were named Weber. The Canadian version, made in Kingston, was taken over by Sherlock-Manning in 1938, and the name was used on many of their pianos until 1968.

Willis (1871-1960) Built (very well) in Montreal. Bought out by Lesage.

Buying a piano

The best piece of advice that anyone can give you before you shop for a new piano is: Pre-qualify yourself first! Know what you want, based on what you need the piano for, and know how much you are prepared to spend.

It's fairly simple to know what you need in the present, but difficult to know what you may need in the future. An upright piano is perfect for those just starting out, and those with limited space or a limited budget, but if you have a musical prodigy in the house, especially if they have reached Grade 10 or above in the

Royal Conservatory of Music Examinations, you will need a grand piano. It is difficult to progress to the upper levels of musicianship on an upright because of one simple fact which I have stated previously: In order for an upright's key to reset to playing position, it must fully return to the up position. A grand key can be replayed even if it is almost fully depressed. This means that a note on a grand piano can repeat much faster, an important feature when playing quickly repeated notes.

With one BIG exception, the size of a piano is an expression of the volume a piano can produce. In a concert hall you need a big piano; in a small room, a big piano could be overwhelming.

The exception to this rule pertains to the smallest upright pianos made, called spinets. In order to make a piano very short, these pianos have an action which is placed below the level of the keyboard, which is called a "Drop-Action". These pianos are suitable for casual entertainment purposes only, and are unsuitable for students that are serious about their studies.

One other important note about size: In order for a piano string to make the correct pitch, it must be the right thickness, the right length, and the right tension. All these factors must be in balance with each other. If you reduce the length, as in a short piano, in order to balance the above factors the string must be made thicker, which affects the tone. Therefore, a bigger piano will not only be louder, but it will have a better tone.

So, now you know what you need in terms of size and type. Next, you must address the inevitable budgetary concerns. In some cases, a used piano might be a very good option if your resources are tight. However, few people would buy a car without having some prior experience in cars, and buying a used piano should be approached in the same way. A used car should be test-driven and safety-checked. Many people also research possible choices, read a "Lemon-Aid" guide, or talk with friends who own the model you are interested in. A used piano should be played by someone who knows pianos, and you should check the seller's track record if commercial. A private seller may not know if the piano they are selling is worth buying. A dealer should know, but, much like the used car trade, there are some shady dealers out there.

There are, however, major differences between a car and a piano. A car has a limited usable lifetime, whereas a piano can last for over a century, passed down from generation to generation. A car loses a substantial amount of its value the moment you drive it off the lot; a piano holds, and in some cases, increases in value. A good used piano, like a good man, is hard to find, but they are out there if you are willing to take your time and look carefully.

If you would prefer to buy a new piano, there is one very important thing to know: It is an unfortunate reality that today's market is flooded with cheap instruments that are a detriment to the budding artist, while decent pianos are often out of reach of the ones that need them. Whether new or used, buy the best instrument you can afford and take care of it. Someday, your great-grandchildren may play it and think of you.

How can you tell if a new piano is a good piano? One of the most important clues is track record. The more experience a builder has, the better they know what they are doing.

For example: W.W. Kimball is an old name in the piano business. He started in 1857, and was once famous for building harmoniums and theatre organs as well as pianos. However, after his death, his son, W.W. Kimball Jr., made increasingly bad business decisions resulting in the company reaching the verge of bankruptcy in 1950. At that point, it was purchased by the Jasper Corporation. The pianos made after that point dropped in quality to the point where, even with re-designing from the ground up and building a new factory in the 1980's, warranty returns and poor sales eventually forced them completely out of the piano business.

It would seem to a piano buyer in 1980 that Kimball had a great track record, having been in business for well over a century, but their actual track record was in fact, terrible. How could a lay-person learn the truth back then? They could ask a piano tuner. Today, of course, all you have to do is search the Internet. Most piano tuners have an e-mail address. Many have websites, and many of those tuners participate in forums.

Just search: "Is Kimball a good piano?" and read the top results. The very best pianos Kimball made while under the Jasper banner were passable pianos. In fact, I have a client who, after I installed new custom-made hammers and completely re-regulated the action from scratch, loves his Kimball. On the other hand, I have many clients who would be happy if they could afford to throw their Kimball on a bonfire. I guarantee that this experience will be repeated online over and over; a few are okay, many are not.

Every piano should receive some level of service by a dealer before it is delivered to you. This "Pre-Delivery Service" should ensure that the piano has no correctable faults and plays the way the builder intended. Even new pianos need some adjustment!

Personally, I would like to see more good old

uprights rebuilt and put in the hands of future pianists, and all new pianos built to a high-quality level. But this isn't going to happen. People will continue to buy what they are buying, dealers will continue to sell what people want, and children will continue to struggle with instruments that do not permit them to learn. To suggest a change to this system would be as anarchistic and as futile as suggesting communism to die-hard capitalists.

Realistically, I can only suggest five things to the prospective first-time piano buyer:

1. Purchase the very best piano you can afford from a reputable dealer that has the facilities to honour their offered warranty.

2. Make sure that your new piano is properly serviced before delivery, and that it is being moved by professional piano movers!

3. Have your piano tuned TWICE a year.

4. Be attentive and involved with your children as they learn.

5. Be willing to reward their progress to higher levels with an instrument that is suitable for their ability.

It is safe to assume that the more money you spend, the better value you will receive. It is my observation that too often, a family buys low because they are unsure as to whether or not their children will stay with the piano. The result of this is that children play on their teacher's piano at their lesson, and then practise on a piano which sounds and feels very different at home. They become frustrated with this incongruity and become discouraged. The parents are then saddled with a piece of furniture, and find it difficult to get their money back.

If a decent piano had been purchased in the first place, it may be that their children would have found the practising easier. If the piano did end up being unused, it would at least have a decent resale value. To avoid being saddled with an unused musical piece of furniture, follow the above rules and find a dealer that will buy-back the piano. Buy-back? Yes, a few dealers will offer this option. Ask your dealer if they will, if they believe in their product, they probably will.

Remember: Out of all the things you possess, your piano is one of the few things that will outlast you, and be lovingly passed down from generation to generation.

How can you tell if you are dealing with a reputable dealer?

1. A new piano's warranty should be included with the invoice, and the dealer should state in writing that they are prepared to carry out warranty repairs themselves without a third party, and without you having to pay any money out yourself. (Some dealers ask you to pay for warranty repairs, and then for you to try to collect from the manufacturer directly.)

2. A used piano should come with a warranty, be clean inside, and in-tune before it is delivered. Any repairs that have to be done to the piano should be inspected by you before delivery.

3. Be very wary of "hole-in-the-wall" dealers who only carry used pianos, or new pianos with unknown names. A sure-fire sign is to ask where the pianos come from. If they say they have a supplier, or that they receive a "truck-load" every few months, run away and don't look back.

I can't stress enough that it is all too common for me to see pianos that should never have been re-sold, and repairs that are unprofessional and counter-productive.

Ten important rules to know before you buy a used piano:

1. It should be clean inside.
2. The hammers shouldn't be grooved where they hit the strings.
3. If the hammers are new, they should be perfectly aligned and evenly spaced.
4. The black keys should not be worn down so that they are rounded, and you should see a tiny flat edge at their front edge, just above and perpendicular to the white keys. When depressed, they should be above the height of the white keys by about the thickness of a nickel.
5. The white keys should be straight and even. (Look along their tops from the side of the piano at eye-level.) They should depress between 10 - 12 mm.
6. When you play the keys, there should be no clicks or buzzes, especially in the bass section.
7. Play a handful of white keys quietly and then quickly lift your hand. There shouldn't be any clicking noises. (Small "thumps" are normal.)

8. The tone should be even, and the piano in-tune.

9. It is always a good idea to consult with your friendly neighbourhood piano tuner.

10. Ideally, it should have a recognizable name. (This is important if you want to re-sell it in the future.)

Please remember the following:

It is extremely rare for an old piano to be valuable. Pianos are not "collectible" items. "Antique" is usually a dirty word. Pianos changed greatly after the First World War, and it is highly unlikely that any used pianos made before 1917 would be a good buy. Even if they have been restored, many of these old pianos have limited value as musical instruments.

Refurbished, reconditioned, rebuilt, and restored are words used very loosely by seller's, but have specific meanings to a qualified technician:

"Refurbished and Reconditioned" are words used to describe a piano that has been repaired to a sellable (and playable) condition. This usually means that the piano has been cleaned, regulated, and tuned, and any broken parts repaired.

"Rebuilt" means the above, plus all worn parts replaced with new parts - including Strings, Tuning Pins, Hammers, Dampers etc.

"Restored" means that the piano has been restored to like new condition in every way.

If any of these phrases have been used by a seller to describe a piano that fail any of the above rules, it is a sign that you should walk away and look somewhere else.

Congratulations! You've bought a piano!

(Or: What to know - before the delivery.)

Before your piano is delivered, plan its placement very carefully. Think of a piano as being part of the family. Pick a room where it will be in the centre of the action. You will want it to be part of celebrations, and most of all, you will want to be able to hear and watch your children practise, and celebrate their accomplishments with them. If the piano is put in a room in the basement where no one wants to go just so it will be played out of ear-shot, I guarantee you that it won't be played.

If you live in a modern, insulated home, it doesn't really matter if it is on a inside or an outside wall. It's far more important that it be as far away as possible from heat registers, windows, and fireplaces. The goal is to put the piano in a position where you, yourself, would be comfortable sitting for a long period of time - someplace where the temperature and humidity is reasonably constant and away from heat sources. Sunshine on your shoulders may make you happy, but it could damage a piano's finish, and the concentrated heat could damage the soundboard and pinblock, leading to costly repairs.

Ideally, an upright piano should be placed so that you can insert your closed fist behind it. This will ensure that the sound will bounce off the wall properly, and it will also allow the tuner to lift the lid without damaging the wall. Try, if possible, to ensure that it is not right up against a side wall either, especially on the right-hand (treble) side. When the tuner is working on this section, having a little room makes the job ten times easier.

Placing a grand piano properly in a room is actually a very tricky thing, and many people have strong feelings about it. If you face the tail into a corner, the player will be facing the wall, and may feel a little isolated. If you face the keys towards a wall, you won't be able to see a player's hands. I personally feel that it's more important to have the keys face outwards. It makes the piano seem more accessible, and certainly makes the tuner's job easier if he or she has to access the action.

A good compromise, though not always

practical, is to have the straight side of the piano against a wall so that the lid opens into the room, the performer can see the audience, and vice-versa. NOTE: Make sure it's not sitting over floor vents!

If you live in an apartment or in a side-by-side, and you're concerned about the sound of the piano disturbing your neighbors, there are a number of simple things that you can do to lessen the transference of sound. First of all, the piano is actually a percussion instrument, and a lot of the sound it transfers is the thumping of the keys. Placing the piano on cushioned castor cups, or on a carpet, will stop a lot of that thumping transferring through the floor. If you have an upright piano that has to be against an adjoining wall, you can get a piece of mattress foam cut to the size of the piano's back, and place it between the piano and the wall.

Many new upright pianos are equipped with a "practice-pedal" which drops a piece of felt between the hammers and the strings. This is a great idea when the player is practising scales and technique, but it's not a good idea to use it constantly when practising. A big part of learning to play the piano is listening to the sounds you are making.

In an apartment block, it's always a good idea to get to know your neighbours, and arrange times when you or your children can play when it won't disturb others. Do this first, and think of it as a way to build community, rather than having to get an angry phone call from the Super after the fact.

If you are lucky enough to not have to worry about the neighbours, and live in a home where the piano can be in a relatively large room, it will sound best if the room has hardwood floors rather than broadloom, but the piano should still be sitting on castor cups.

If you think that you may need to shift the piano's position every once and a while, you could arrange to have the piano's metal wheels replaced with rubber-wheeled castors, although this detracts a bit from the look of a grand.

One more important fact about the piano's "wheels": They are not made for rolling the piano around. They are designed for small movements only - pulling an upright away from a wall, shifting a grand a few inches to the left or the right. If you want the piano to be truly movable, it must be fitted with proper rubber-wheeled castors, or in the case of a grand piano, either a tripod or leg dollies.

If you do have to shift an upright, there are handles on the back for one hand, and the other hand should be on the front of the keyboard. Never push an upright piano backwards holding the piano near the top - it could tip backwards, causing injury to yourself, or worse, to the piano. If your piano has free front legs that are not connected to the bottom of the piano, try to lift slightly on the keyboard as you move. These legs are known to snap off, toppling the piano forward.

If you have to shift a grand, it's highly recommended that you use three strong people: two on each side of the keyboard, and one big brute on the tail end. Be very careful if running over carpet or bumps on the floor. It is not unheard of for one or more of the legs to snap off, bringing the piano crashing to the floor.

Once again, any moving of more than a foot should be done by professional movers unless the piano is specially equipped.

Care and... feeding?

When I was little, I would wake up every Sunday morning to the sound of my mother dusting the piano. Of course, she was dusting everything (being my mom), but nothing else in the house made that familiar badum, badum, badum sound of her cleaning the keys.

You might say that cleaning runs in the family: Not only did my mother keep a spotless house (even though she worked full-time – I'll tell you her secret in a second), but her youngest brother, my uncle Stan, owned a cleaning company.

I worked for Uncle Stan during the summer break when I was fifteen. He taught me two things: Have a system, and work to an end. I took to working with him like a duck takes to water because...

I Love Cleaning.

Therein lies the secret to my mom's clean house - she had me as a son. As I say in my book, "Dear Mr. Musselwhite...":

"My mother used to call me Mr. Clean... because if she gave me a job, I would do it to an extreme. If she asked me to dust, I would take apart the lamps and fixtures to clean inside them. If I was asked to tidy, I would rearrange all the books on the shelves in alphabetical order. To my parent's chagrin, this dedication never did extend to school work."

I have cleaned many, many pianos since those early years, and I can say without a hint of Braggadocio that I know how to do it, and I'm pleased to be able to share the secret with you:

Get me to do it.

No, seriously, you can do a lot yourself, and it's not difficult nor time-consuming. Leave the inside to a pro, but you can do the rest yourself.

The first thing you need to know is what kind of finish your piano has. If you just bought your piano brand new, you can ask the dealer, but chances are great that it is finished in polyester.

Polyester is a synthetic polymer similar to plastic. It was first used as a piano finish by the European builders starting in the late 1970's, but its use has spread to almost all of the new pianos being made.

It's very hard, adheres to wood like a glue, (because, basically, it is a kind of glue), and can be polished to a mirror-like reflection, or rubbed with special abrasives to make a silky satin sheen. It's also highly toxic to produce and to apply, but who am I to judge?

You can tell if your piano is finished in polyester by finding a hidden part, like inside the kickboard or the bottom of the bench seat, and make a tiny scrape with a razor blade. If it's polyester, the scratch and the shavings will be white.

You can clean polyester with plain old water, or Windex if it's really dirty, but the secret is to wet a soft cloth (NOT the piano), and use a dry soft cloth right after to polish it. If you want a high polish, there are specific polishes made just for a poly finish.

If there are scratches or chips in the finish, a refinisher, specializing in polyester, can remove them. A few hours with a polishing machine in skilled hands can make a piano finished in polyester looking brand new. That's the beauty of it.

If your piano was made before the 1980's, but after the 1930's, it's probably finished in Nitrocellulose Lacquer. Remember the little scrape you made to test the finish? Lacquer scratches clear.

Lacquer has the advantage of being repairable with just a little training and with minimal tools. It can even be bought in non-toxic water-based form, for green people.

Although lacquer can have a gloss shine, it doesn't match the depth and clarity of polyester, and it is a little tricky to apply it to raw wood. Its main drawback is that it is extremely sensitive to damage, and especially sensitive to water and other liquids.

If your piano is finished in lacquer, keep liquids away from it. Don't use your piano as a drink coaster, or a display shelf for your flowers. If it does get even a little drop of water on it, dry it off immediately.

It's a good idea to be careful with everything

you put on it because it can be temperamental. It's possible, under the right circumstances, for the finish to soften enough so that paper will stick to it, or, conversely, for it to become brittle enough to chip.

The secret to cleaning a lacquer finish is to not have to. Dust the piano often using a feather duster, and if you have to remove a smudge or a blot, use a slightly damp cloth, followed by a dry soft cloth.

If there is a large build up of dust, use a slightly damp cloth, quickly drying with a soft dry cloth. If it is really dirty, or if there is some kind of build up, use a little "Murphy's Oil Soap" with warm (not hot) water in a bucket, wring the cloth out well, and do small areas at a time. Follow with clean cool water, and dry immediately. DO NOT RUB HARD!

Never use any kind of over-the counter polishes like Pledge or Endust. I would also not recommend using any oils or polishes either, because although they may make the piano look shiny, it can cause the finish to soften, and can build up into a wax that is hard to remove.

Before the advent of lacquer, pianos were finished in French-polished shellac. This is an ancient, difficult finish to apply, but done properly, it is literally the most beautiful finish that you have ever seen – shinier than polyester, clear like glass, and creating an illusion of depth, as if you are looking through a coating of water.

If applied and cared for properly, French polish finishes can last for centuries. Go visit a museum if you don't believe me. Although beautiful, it's a very complicated and demanding finish to apply. It protects wood so well that it actually preserves it, but it is also fragile, and very sensitive to abuse, humidity, extreme dryness, and temperature fluctuations.

If French polish is so great, why do so many old pianos look so terrible? It's because they haven't been properly cared for. Before I tell you how, I'll tell you the incredibly interesting story behind French Polishing.

The Incredibly Interesting Story Behind French Polishing

French polishing originated in the early 18th century, but its roots date back to many centuries before. The main ingredient in the finish is shellac, which the Europeans "discovered", during their nasty little visits to the East.

Shellac is made from the dried sweat of the Female Lac Beetle, which lives in certain trees in India and Thailand. For many centuries, village children were employed collecting the branches and bark of these trees which would be laid out in the village square to dry.

The children would then have a merry time in the hot sun, stamping on this collection, wearing flat-bottomed wooden sandals, until everything was ground down to smallish chunks.

This would then be swept up and put into large pierced drums which would be turned over and over until a fine powder could be collected. The powder was then boiled until all that remained was a flaky resin.

Depending on the type of tree, the resin flakes could be anything from a very light yellow, to a dark smoky brown. Mixed with alcohol or other agents, the resin could be made into a variety of products, ranging from liquid shellac, to a mold-able material almost like glass. In fact, the early Victrola records were first made from shellac.

To French polish, many thin layers of shellac are rubbed on by hand in a manner that not only spreads it thinly, but polishes it as it is applied. French polishing even a small piece can take many hours, so you can imagine how long, and how hard it was to apply it on to a large object such as a piano.

It's no wonder, then, that piano makers were so quick to jump onto the lacquer bandwagon. Today, French polishing is all but a lost art.

More than likely, if your piano was French polished, you will see the effects of improper care on the finish. Old shellac finishes will have either a network of tiny cracks, or if it's really bad, an effect known as leathering, where the finish has dried to the point where there are more cracks than not, and the surface literally looks like old leather.

If the finish was applied well, all one would have to do to make sure that it forever looks like new would be to keep it out of the sun, away from liquids, and regularly moisturize it with lemon oil. If your piano is just starting to show the signs of drying out, buy REAL lemon oil (not a polish WITH lemon oil), apply the oil to a soft cloth, spread it over the finish, let sit for a few minutes, and then wipe it off with a clean, dry, soft cloth.

If the finish is so bad that it has leathered, lemon oil might help a little, but chances are, to make it look new, it will have to be refinished.

Cleaning the Keys

In general, the technique to clean both Ivory and Plastic keytops are the same: Spray a soft cloth with a little water or Windex, clean a small section at a time, and dry immediately with a dry cloth. Make sure you clean the sides of the black keys.

Now, having said everything above, I should tell you that all you really need to do on a regular basis, is dust with a Swiffer or feather duster, and wipe the keys from the back to the front with a soft cloth.

Do this once a week, and you'll only need to seriously clean your piano once a year. (Unless, of course, someone has dirty fingers, or an accident.) That's it!

If you have ivory keytops, don't close the keycover unless you need to protect them against mauraders. Ivory yellows if not exposed to light. Plastic, on the other hand, especially the plastic keys made in the 1960's to the 1980's can turn yellowish if not kept covered.

By the way, the main reason that keys get chipped is because something has been used to depress them other than fingers, ex: a toy car, or a G.I. Joe. Please remind every little pianist: "Fingers only on the keys, no toys, or feet, or elbows please!"

The Top Five Reasons to Tune Your Piano regularly:

5. Piano strings are steel wires under a tremendous amount of pressure, and they stretch.

The piano has 88 notes, but many of the notes have more than one string. In fact, an average piano has approximately 240 strings. All these strings add up to around 14 or more tons of pressure. Over time, and with the added pressure of being struck to sound a note, the strings will stretch and go out of tune. This is especially true of new pianos, and pianos that have been re-strung or rebuilt.

4. Wood reacts to humidity changes. When it is damp, it swells; when it is dry, it shrinks.

All these tightened strings rest across a piece of wood called a "Bridge" which is glued to the soundboard. This is how the sound of the strings is amplified. The soundboard is slightly arched, and is glued tightly to the perimeter of the piano. When the ambient humidity increases, the arch increases and stretches the strings more, making the pitch sharp.

When the humidity decreases, the arch decreases, making the pitch flat.

3. The pitch of a piano (the tension of the strings) is not arbitrary. The piano must be kept at proper pitch in order to sound the way that the manufacturer intended.

The pitch of a string (the note it sounds) is determined by three factors: the thickness of the string, the length of the string, and the tension. If you look inside a piano, you will notice that the strings are all a different length. This measurement cannot be changed, neither can the thickness of the string. These two factors were set by the manufacturer, therefore, the only variable is the tension. As the piano goes out of tune, each string will not only be off-pitch, but off-tone as well.

2. A piano that is tuned regularly stays in tune longer.

Your piano was designed to be at a specific pitch: "Concert Pitch" or A:440 (This means that the note A above middle C vibrates at 440 beats per second). If you let your piano cycle through more than one season change, the above factors will cause it to go so flat, that the piano tuner will have to stretch the strings sharp before tuning it at A:440. This is called a pitch raise. It is usually twice the cost of a normal tuning, is hard on the piano, and results in a tuning that is not as stable. A piano that is regularly tuned will stay close to pitch and will not need a pitch raise.

The Most Important Reason Of Them All:

1. A properly tuned piano is essential for good musicianship.

Young students will be greatly hampered in their studies if their piano is not kept in tune. They will notice the difference between their piano and their teacher's piano, and it will confuse them. It will also interfere with ear training. Worst of all, you may become accustomed to the sound of an out-of-tune piano, so that the sound of a good piano, in concert or recording, may sound strange. One thing is certain: It will be impossible for your children to progress far in their studies if they have to practise on a poor instrument, or even on a good instrument if it is not in tune.

An alphabetical guide to a few common piano repairs and adjustments

Bridge Repair: The "Bridge" is a long curved piece of wood that is glued to the soundboard. The strings pass over top of the bridge, guided by small pins. It is this direct connection that allows the vibration of the strings to be transmitted to the soundboard, which amplifies the sound.

Sometimes, due to environmental causes, age, or poor construction, the cap on top of the bridge cracks, and the pins become loose. This causes the sound of the strings to become indistinct or "buzzy". To correct this, the cap must be repaired or replaced, and the pins replaced, or glued and tightly re-glued.

Cleaning: When dirt or oil accumulates on the strings, the sound they make becomes dull sounding or "tubby". Sometimes, the sound of older strings can be improved by cleaning. The treble, or plain-wire strings, are cleaned by rubbing them with steel wool or a nylon scouring pad. The bass strings, which are wound with copper or iron, are loosened one at a time and removed from the bottom part of the piano. Then they are vigourously rubbed with steel wool or a nylon scouring pad. Lastly, the strings are curled upon themselves and bent back and forth to remove dirt between the windings. The rest of the back and belly of the piano is usually cleaned after the above procedure to remove any dirt that was loosened by string cleaning. In a grand piano, the soundboard is cleaned using a soft cloth and a soundboard steel - a flat, thin, and flexible strip of steel which guides a dusting cloth underneath the strings.

The action and keybed naturally collect a lot of dust. Although this does not usually cause technical problems, cleanliness is next to godliness and is a normal part of piano maintenance. Rodents and insects often nest under the keys, which damages the wood and felt. Placing a few small cakes of Irish Spring soap under the keys and in the bottom of the piano is thought to repel mice in a safe and environmentally friendly manner.

Bridge Pin Resetting: The bridge pins can be given a tap to ensure tightness in the bridge. This helps to correct "False Beats" in strings, giving the tone of the strings more clarity.

Coil Tightening: The strings coil around the tuning pins at the top of their run. This coil must be tight together to ensure tuning stability.

String and Loop Bedding: The strings must lay tightly across the bridge and not "hang up" on the pin. At the bottom of the string, the loop that goes around the final anchor must also be tight against the plate.

Tightening of all Screws, Nuts, and Bolts: All the fasteners must be tight to ensure that the piano is stable and solid. Because of the wooden rails expanding and contracting as the humidity levels rise and fall, the action screws should be periodically tightened.

Re-gluing Ribs: Don't worry too much if you have a crack in your soundboard. This in itself is not important. What is important is that the ribs glued to the back of the soundboard are tight against the board at the place of the crack. If the soundboard has pulled away from the rib, they must be re-glued to ensure that the board will not buzz or rattle.

Repinning: If the tuning pins are too loose to hold the string in tune, they can be replaced with a slightly larger pin. Before this is done, the technician should ensure that the pinblock is in good shape and solid, that the strings still have enough elasticity not to break when unwound, and that the soundboard and ribs are tightly glued.

Tuning Pin Re-setting: If the tuning pins are a little loose, they may be given a hard tap, which gives the pins new wood in the pinblock to grab and hold.

Centre Pin Replacement: All the moving parts in the action rotate on small silver-coated brass pins that are held tightly by felt bushings. When these pins become loose in the bushings, parts can click when moving, the hammers can flop sideways when hitting the strings causing indistinct tone, and this can cause undue wear. To correct this, the pin is replaced with a larger size, and the bushing slightly reamed to remove wear and grease.

Key Bushing Replacement: Small chrome-plated brass pins guide the movement of the piano keys on the key frame. These pins contact strips of felt inside the key known as bushing cloth. When this wears, the keys wiggle side-to-side, increasing unwanted noise, and decreasing the player's comfort. New felt is glued in to replace the worn bushings.

Keytop Replacement and Polishing: If the keytops are very dirty, scratched, or dull, a technician can remove the keys, clean them, and then polish them with a buffing wheel.

If the keytops are broken or cracked, new plastic keytops can be applied to renew the piano's appearance. A good technician will always shape each key individually, and smooth and polish all the edges. It is sometimes possible to replace one or two chipped ivories, but the supply of these parts is becoming more and more limited.

Re-bending of the springs: The proper working of an upright action depends on the tension of two finger springs and one coil spring. Re-bending the finger springs renews their ability to function properly.

Re-lubrication of friction points: There are many points of friction inside a piano's action. Some are metal on felt; some are wood on leather. Over time, the original lubrication wears off and must be replaced.

Replacement of the Bridle Straps: The hammers, after striking the strings, return to rest by the action of a spring, and by the weight of the whippen. The two parts are connected by a small strip of cloth called a bridle strap. The straps have an average lifetime of forty to fifty years, and must be replaced when worn out.

Replacement of the Jack Springs: This internal coil spring becomes weak with age and use, and often causes the keys to cease functioning. Replacement with brand new springs often makes a surprising difference in the "touch" of the keys.

Re-shaping of the Hammers: What with all the repetitive pounding of the strings, the hammers wear deep grooves in their striking points. This causes the tone to become uneven and impure. The hammers themselves are made from multiple layers of hard felt wrapped around a wooden core. To re-shape them, a technician removes a few layers, ensuring all the time that the proper shape of the hammer is maintained. A well-shaped hammer has a very small striking point - smaller than the tip of your little finger!

Tightening of all screws: Every screw in the action must be tight to eliminate noise and undue wear.

Regulation: Regulation is a collection of procedures that ensures that all parts of the keyboard and action work correctly together. A piano's mechanism is very complex - over three thousand individual parts! Many of these parts have tiny adjustment points that must be set properly so that the piano sounds and plays like it was designed to. A piano's action is like a large and complex handmade cuckoo clock. Every little piece must work properly in order for the clock to keep the correct "time".

Castor Replacement: The castors or wheels supplied by the manufacturer are usually not designed with moving a piano around in mind. They allow the piano to be moved a little - away from a wall for cleaning - for example, but no more than a foot or two. They are small iron wheels with no bearings or cushions. They simply hold the piano off the floor. Often they break, and cause the piano to tilt. I recommend that every piano should have new ball-bearing rubber castors retro-fitted (if practicable) to make shifting a piano easier and safer.

Pedal Replacement: Damage by movers or by dropping the bench can cause one or more pedals to break in half. Because they are made from cast iron, welding is usually not a practical way of repairing them. Replacing broken pedals with new ones is much more time - and cost-efficient.

NOTE: All too often, piano pedals are broken when someone attempts to lift the bench lid from the wrong side, causing the bench to fall over on top of the pedals. An easy way to prevent this is to orient the bench so that the bench hinges face the piano.

When I was little, one of my first jobs in my dad's store was to turn the benches the right way around!

Pedal Re-plating: Re-plating with nickel or chrome can renew old, worn, and tarnished pedals. This is a relatively simple and inexpensive procedure that works wonders in improving a piano's appearance.

Spring Replacement: With age and wear, the springs that return the pedal to their "up" position may break. Replacing these springs with new ones restores the pedal's function.

Pitch Raising: If the piano hasn't been tuned in a long time, or if it has been moved and stored, it may need a quick additional tuning to bring it up to pitch.

Real Life Questions and Answers

Q: I have a new baby grand, but I feel the humidity has affected my piano. The pitch is always flat, and the keys and the pedals squeak, too!

A: New pianos always need a little "breaking-in" period. However, it's possible that your piano was not properly serviced before delivery. All new pianos require some adjustment when they arrive from the factory, regulation of the action, seating of the strings, and proper lubrication of certain moving parts.

If the piano was pre-serviced, it's possible that you have a humidity fluctuation problem in your home. If the humidity is not fairly constant, it could be causing some of your problems. You can buy something called a "Dammp-Chaser" that will keep its internal humidity levels at an optimum 42%. It can only be installed by a qualified technician, but it is very easy to operate. A little panel of three lights (installed just under the keyboard) tells you that it is on, lets you know when to add water, and if it needs servicing. For more information, visit www.pianolifesaver.com.

-o-

Q: I was just wondering... in terms of the tone of my piano, I know it sounds more mellow than other pianos out there. I was wondering if it's possible to make it sound 'brighter'?

A: Certainly! Piano hammers, especially new-ish ones, can be made softer or brighter by a process called Voicing. Hammers are made with layers upon layers of densely-packed felt, wrapped around a wooden molding. The felt layers can be made stiffer, or softer, by a qualified piano technician, right in your home.

If the hammers are very old or worn, they can be replaced with new ones, which are very easy to adjust in terms of tone. Normally, the older and more worn a hammer gets, the brighter it becomes, so it probably just needs normal voicing.

-o-

Q: I'd like a good family piano - one that will be played and enjoyed - but not by experts - strictly for recreation. It will, I hope, be the focal point of the living room and family gatherings. Both children have now exceeded the capacity of my old Clavinova, and they really need a decent instrument on which to learn.

A: Congratulations! You're making the right decision. I especially like that you want your new piano to be the centre of attention!

A digital piano is either a tool, or a toy. It's great for late night practising using headphones or plugging into your computer to record. Plus, all the bells and whistles are popular with the child in all of us.

When learning to play the piano, especially if your are taking lessons and taking the Royal Conservatory of Music examinations, you need a real piano in order to progress. My advice is that you figure out how much you are willing to spend, and then buy the best piano you can afford. It's better to buy a great apartment-size upright, then a cheap baby grand.

Take your family and visit one of your local, large, well-established piano retailers, and see what your options are. If you have any questions, please feel free to e-mail me.

-o-

Q: I'd like to buy a small grand (5' or so), preferably with a mahogany finish, but I would consider black. I've looked at new Samick's, Remingtons, Kohler/Campbells (which I understand are all the same company), and Nordheimer. But, honestly, I am confused. Each salesperson has told me reasons why I should not buy the competing brand! Is there really any difference between any of the major brands? After all, they're all factory-produced in Asia!

A: Grr. My father always told me: "Don't speak ill of the competition!" Salespeople should always try to tell you the selling points of their products without casting aspersions on others.

The truth is that there are many "Asian" countries producing pianos, and they are not all equal. With a few exceptions, the cost of labour is the best indication of quality.

My father was one of the first Canadian dealers to import pianos from Japan, only a decade after the second World War. Back then, "Made In Japan" meant cheap, and I'm sure you would agree that this perception has changed radically.

Once the Japanese piano makers started to get a great reputation, in order to keep the prices of their economy models low, they shifted production to South Korea. Once the Korean companies started to get a good reputation, pianos started to be made in Indonesia, and now, China.

I have two pieces of advice: Buy the best piano you can afford, and buy from a dealer that you feel you can trust. As for your experience with salespeople, don't invite them to stray into negative territory by asking them about pianos that they don't sell. Instead, ask them about the pianos that they are featuring.

One last little tip: This sounds a little funny, but it's the truth. Don't just listen to a salesperson's words – listen to the emotion. Every one of them knows which pianos they love, and which they are required to sell. Try to find which is which by being sensitive to them! Remember that although it is their job to sell pianos, if it's a career choice, they really don't want to steer you wrong. Every customer they disappoint means many other potential customers will avoid them in the future.

-o-

Q: I have a Heintzman 6'7" grand. Can I buy a replacement key cover for a 'D' note (2 below C)? If it's not too much trouble, I'd like to get just that one for now, although I would like to have the whole set eventually redone.

A: I can put on a replacement, but chances are that it won't match. If you need an ivory keytop, there is a HUGE variation in colour, grain, and size. I might be able to find something that is close, but it won't be perfect. There are variations in plastic, as well. I don't keep used plastic key-tops in stock, and a new one will undoubtedly be a lot whiter than the original.

By the way, I should put it on for you. You can't just stick them on – ivories need special preparation, glue, and a special clamp, and plastic has to be custom shaped.

–o–

Q: We have an old square piano that we would like you to take a look at.

A: Well, you've asked the right guy. I've worked on many over the years, and not only is the experience helpful (they're incredibly different from regular pianos), but I actually have all of my grandfather's tools for doing the job.

I should just give you a little heads-up: When was the last time it was tuned? Square pianos, unless very well-maintained or properly rebuilt, are often untuneable. It may need more than just tuning!

-o-

Q: Have you ever heard of a Gordon Laughead piano?

A: To be honest, I haven't. There are thousands and thousands of makes out there, many just made by a small company that made only a few. It sounds from the name, that it might be a British "Cottage Industry" piano. There were few of these pianos made and brought over, and although that means it's rare, it doesn't mean that it's good. The best thing to do? Have me over to look at it. Perhaps at tea-time!

-o-

Q: I recently bought a piano on eBay and picked it up a couple days ago. I think it is about 40 to 50 years old, and it is a Nordheimer, made in

Toronto. There are quite a few things wrong with it and I was hoping for a quote to fix it. Here is the list:

3 broken hammer shanks (I have the hammer heads)
4 broken wires (strings)
12 broken bridle straps
1 broken wire that retracts damping mechanism
Major tuning is required

I was hoping you can give me a rough estimate (within 100 dollars).

A: I don't charge for on-site repair estimates, so it would be best if I could come over and see it. However, chances are that it has more than just the problems you've described. Piano strings usually last longer than 40 – to 50 years. If more than one is broken, it's possible that the strings are corroded, and more may break when I tune it. Twelve broken bridle straps almost certainly means that all of them should be replaced. The broken damper spring that you mention might mean that the springs are fatigued.

Are you certain that it is as young as you think? Nordheimer pianos during the 1960's were smallish apartment-size pianos made by Heintzman, and the decal usually says: "Nordheimer by Heintzman". If you've lifted the lid and looked inside, it will say

"Heintzman" as well.

It's very possible that it is almost twice that age. Nordheimer's of that age were great pianos, but pianos age as people do, and it might be an old man with health problems. Luckily, pianos can be re-built (unlike old men).

-o-

Q: I would like to get castors for my Heintzman. Are the originals brass or plain steel or rubber? How much would they cost? I want to get rid of the spider that I have now and get it back on castors with a carpet underneath for sound absorption.

A: Because you mentioned that your piano is on a spider dolly, I'm assuming it's a grand. The standard grand castor is brass, but there is no standard in size or mounting. It's unfortunate, but the only way to tell is to come over with some burly men, take the piano off the dolly, and put it on its side. The legs will have to be removed and the new castors made to fit the original mounts. You are looking at a fee for my labour, the cost of the movers, and the price of the new casters.

-o-

Q: We have a Behr Bros. #165324. What can you tell us about its age and value?

A: Your piano was made right at the end of the Great Depression of the 1930's. It was actually made by Kohler and Campbell, who bought Behr Brothers in 1910. It's not the greatest piano in the world, made during one of the worst periods in piano making, and unfortunately, probably isn't worth much on the market. It may still have life left in it, though, but I would have to see it to tell you about its true condition. By the way, a little bit of trivia: Kohler and Campbell's original piano factory was demolished to make Central Park!

-o-

Q: I would like to learn how to repair and tune a piano. I have a book from the library which explains repair and regulation. Is there a course in the Toronto area that I could take? What would you recommend? Thank you kindly for your advice.

A: Are you sure you wouldn't want to learn something simpler like Brain Science, or Rocket Surgery? The only reason for going into this business is that you love pianos. If that's the case, The University of Western Ontario offers a two-year program in piano Technology. After that course is completed, the best thing to do would be to get a job in a piano shop where you can have the opportunity to learn from others, and get some real hands-on experience.

Q: I just finished my piano-tuning course and am looking for a job in piano tuning. Are you hiring right now ?

A: It's been well over a decade since I had a shop big enough to hire employees and apprentices, and I don't envision going that route in the future. However, that is exactly what you need. Write every piano store and rebuilder that you can find in your area, tell them who you are, what you can do, and impress them with your work ethic and personality. Eventually, you'll find the perfect place. Good Luck!

-o-

Q: Rather than picking up something cheap in desperate need of repair, I've been advised to check with a piano tuner about the availability of reconditioned pianos. Do you know of any?

A: Although I do run across them once in a while, in general, all I can offer you are pianos that I have rebuilt, and are for sale. They are generally about the same price as a new piano, so that might not be what you are looking for.

There are two options open to you: Go to a respectable retailer and see what they have to offer, or look on-line. Either way, shop carefully. Let me know what you are considering before you buy, and ask my advice. I'm happy to oblige!

-o-

Q: I found a circa 1905 Bell upright the other week, and it has an "Illimitable Repeating Action". What does that mean?

A: The "aught's" were the time of experimentation for piano builders, and Bell was no exception. They tried a number of new ideas, many of which were fantastic, but it meant that their pianos were very different from the norm and more expensive to make. It eventually did them in. They made great pianos, but when the Depression hit, few could afford their higher price.

One of their inventions, the "Illimitable Action", was an attempt to duplicate in an upright one of the main benefits of a grand. This action had an extra spring which would allow the note to be repeated without the key being fully released. It worked well, but it is fragile. The spring is attached to a small loop of silk, which wears and breaks, and is very difficult to replace. Many (ahem) "technicians" cut the thing out instead of fixing it. To re-install it after it is cut is worth literally thousands of dollars; repairing it instead is only about six hours of labour. But, that's six hours that most people won't pay for, as the action works fine without it.

-o-

Q: I would like to refinish my piano myself. Do you have any tips and pointers you can give me?

A: Yes. Don't do it. Not only is it a big, difficult, and messy job, but, unless you know how to take the piano apart and put it back together again, you'll end up making a mess of it. It's not like a table or a chair – a piano is a complicated and heavy thing with a lot of surface area to deal with – much of it hidden behind parts that have to be removed to refinish.

If you really want to do it, go see what professionals have to do in order to do a good job. You might get a useful tip, such as: "Don't do it yourself."

-o-

Q: I was looking up pianos on the computer and was fortunate to find you. How I wish I had come across your website before I purchased my new baby grand piano! I am retired and several years ago I had to break up my home and sell my Steinway baby grand piano. I have tried to get used to this piano, however, I guess I was disappointed after having a Steinway for so many years.

A piano is a very personal thing and it takes time and a great deal of hunting to find the right one. I wish I had known you before I bought the one I have. It seems today you are expected to just go in and buy something. There is not much dialogue or advice given.

The piano doesn't seem to keep in tune for very long. Is this our climate? Some dampers had to be aligned, some easing, tighten some loose screws, some tight hammer centres lubricated, etc. Can you give me any advice?

A: Well, my dear, you're dealing with two things here: A new piano which needs a little TLC and settling in, and Buyer's Remorse.

Buyer's remorse is very common. A piano is a big investment, and many people worry, after the piano has arrived, that they have made a mistake. In general, however, they grow to love the piano, and it becomes a part of the family. And, if children learn on it, they'll look at "the old girl" with great fondness, and happy memories.

Certainly, any piano that replaces your dear old Steinway has a lot to live up to, and although it's entirely possible that it will never be as dear to you, don't give up on the new one yet. I can take a look and see if I can address some of your complaints.

-o-

Q: I just came across your website while trying to find out some history about a pianola I just bought, and I was hoping you might be able to help me. It's labelled: Gourlay, Toronto, Canada. It says on the piano back that it was made specifically for the Australian and New Zealand climates. The serial number is: 104437. I bought it on an online auction a week ago for $100 (NZ). The poor old thing has had a hard life. For some strange reason it was covered in sand, and bird poo! But, I've cleaned it up, and I think it's going to be okay. The piano itself plays fine, but is in need of a tune. However, the pianola doesn't appear to be working. If you could tell me a bit about its history, it would be much appreciated.

A: Sand and bird poo? You didn't perchance find it on a beach just after they finished filming the movie "The Piano", did you? Gourlay was a piano retailer in Toronto from 1890 to 1923, and built pianos as Gourlay, Winter and Leeming from 1904 until 1923 when they went into receivership. Sherlock Manning bought them out in 1924.

The Pianola player mechanism is probably in need of complete rebuilding. It relies on many parts that age poorly and often disintegrate. It's a very expensive process that few technicians are capable of, requiring over 80 hours of labour, and hundreds of dollars in parts. It would be cheaper to rip the thing out and replace it with the modern version, called a Pianodisc. Not only is it superior in every way, you don't have to pump it. Check it out: www.pianodisc.com.

The decal saying that it was made for a specific climate is an old sales gimmick. The fact is, that between Austrailia and New Zealand, there is everything from desert to rainforest and everything in between. It's kind of like saying: "Built for the North American Climate". Which one? Inuvik? Victoria? Las Vegas? Miami?

One thing's for sure - it wasn't built to be a bird's nest!

-o-

Q: I am wondering if you are able to fix a problem I am having with my piano. The B above middle C doesn't work properly, and rings on after you release the key.

A: Of course I can! It's probably a very quick repair. More than likely the damper spring has slipped off. It's possible that it might be something else, but there's only one way to know for sure - invite me over.

Hope to see you soon!

Top Ten Things To Know About The Piano

1. Anyone can learn to play the piano!

2. A piano can be a surprisingly good investment. Out of all the things you possess, your piano is one of the few things that will outlast you, and will be lovingly passed down from generation to generation.

3. Different pianos are suitable for different needs.

4. Don't judge a piano by its case. A beautiful outside may hide a myriad of problems.

5. A piano should be moved by professionals, not by you and a few friends.

6. Ideally, a piano should be by an inside wall in a poorly insulated home, away from all heat sources, and in a room where it can be part of the family.

7. Different piano finishes must be cared for in different ways.

8. Pianos are affected by changes in temperature and humidity.

9. A piano should be tuned at least once a year, but twice a year is best!

10. A piano is meant to be played, not to be a piece of furniture.

Afterword

When I was sixteen, my father and I took a car trip out to Vancouver Island. Even though my Mom and Dad owned and operated a large music store, he always took time off in the summer and did something special with me.

While in Vancouver, he stopped in at a store to visit with one of his many friends in the piano business. I took the opportunity to pop into the guitar shop next door.

At the time, I thought that I was the hottest sixteen-year-old guitarist in the country. I didn't really have any basis for that belief, but nevertheless, I still thought I was mighty good.

While I was looking for a suitable axe to pick up and wail on, a little boy, not more than nine or ten, walked in, picked up a Stratocaster, and played things I hadn't even imagined.

Totally disillusioned, I walked out, sat in the car and waited for my dad to return. Although I was feeling very depressed, I tried to put on a brave face for my dad when he returned.

"So, did you find a nice guitar to play?" he aske,d as he settled into his seat.

"Not really," I replied. "How was your friend?"

"He has a beautiful store!" he said, his face lighting up. "Great pianos, a great shop, everything a piano man could ask for."

It seemed as though perhaps my dad had just had a similar experience, and I sat in silence for a while thinking about what he had just said.

"Is it better than yours?" I asked.

Dad looked at me quizzically for a moment – a puzzled, almost sad expression on his face.

"Son," he finally answered, "nobody ever has anything better than what you have. The most anybody can have is something different. I have no idea what it took for him to get where he is, but I bet it wasn't a cakewalk."

I learned many things from my dad, much of it not about pianos. However, everything is related.

"Never envy anybody else," he told me. "Many people have it a lot worse."

Although I often see piano tuners that need a lot of improvement, I constantly meet tuners whose skills are much greater than mine. One of the best things about this career is that there is always room for improvement.

In a job where problem-solving, compromise, and patience are the key skills needed, you can never rest on your laurels and think you know it all. It just isn't possible.

Every day brings a new piano, and with it, a new challenge. Whether you're just starting to tune, or have been tuning for decades, I sincerely hope that this book has helped to kindle (or re-kindle) an interest and a passion for "The Art of Compromise".

James (Jamie) Musselwhite.

About the Author...

Jamie Musselwhite grew up among the sound of pianos and piano tuning. His father, Caleb Henry (Cal) Musselwhite, and his grandfather, Fredrick William, were both piano technicians, and today, he and his brother, John, carry on the family tradition.

For close to a half-century, Jamie has tuned, repaired and rebuilt pianos professionally, but his love of pianos stems from being a young boy literally learning at the knee of his father.

Jamie has tuned for orchestras, ballet and opera companies, and universities in Victoria, Calgary, Saskatoon, Winnipeg and Toronto, and for artists as diverse as Anton Kuerti, Victor Borge, The Pointer Sisters, Burton Cummings and Alice Cooper.

Although he was born and raised a prairie boy, Jamie now lives in Toronto, Canada.

James Musselwhite

"The Art of Compromise"

Second Edition © 2018 James Musselwhite

www.torontopianotuning.com

Made in the USA
Coppell, TX
03 July 2024

34216268R00138